Stone of Help

Ebenezer:

The First Fifty Years

(1911 – 1961)

Edited by Marilyn C. Maye, Ed.D.

First Printing, 2011

Copyright © 2011 by Marilyn C. Maye

All rights reserved.

ISBN: 0-9675400-1-1
ISBN-13: 978-0-9675400-1-6

FaithWorks

Bronx, New York

F8thWorks@aol.com

DEDICATION

This book is dedicated to the memory of all of those who came to a strange city and erected a Stone of Help, that has shaped generations and is still changing the world.

CONTENTS

Acknowledgments i

Introduction 3

Contributors 7

Part 1

The American Context 11

The Caribbean Immigrant Context 19

The Holiness Revival Context 39

Part 2

Memoirs 53

Legacies 105

Photographs 113

Afterword 117

Notes 119

Acknowledgments

Special thanks are due:

To Warren L. Maye, Dr. Grace Allman Burke, Rev. Gloria W. Nurse, and Angela Vassel for their invaluable advice, encouragement, and editorial assistance throughout this project

To all who took the time to pen their memories: Luther Allman, Dr. Grace Burke, Hon. Carl O. Callender, Dr. Clive Callender, Olwen Gillman, Gloria Johnson, Roxanne Kent, Rev. Gloria W. Nurse, Dorothy Oliver, Edith Rock, and Waldo Waterman.

To Edwina Nelbett, Beverly Oliver, and Lynette Rock for facilitating their mothers' memoirs.

To Jesus Christ, the Helper, who made all of these stories possible, and whom the memorial stone calls us to remember.

Introduction

STONE OF HELP is a story of a small group of ordinary people who, using a stone memorial as their trademark, built a faith community that has lasted 100 years. They were part of the African Diaspora, and they came to New York City in the early 1900s, in search of a better life. They achieved that goal, for themselves and countless others, by establishing Ebenezer Gospel Tabernacle of the Christian Mission of the U.S.A. Born late in the 19th century and now deceased, those pioneers still speak into the 21st century, through the memories of the contributors to this volume who knew them personally.

We write for you who have come of age in a new millennium, and who may sometimes question why you stay in church at all. We want to leave you stories about a generation who, at your age, 'lit a candle rather than cursed the darkness.' We want you to know that you are spiritual descendants of heroes and sheroes, and that you too can shine a light into dark places in your world, and make a difference that can last a century. They lived through two world wars, a horrific flu pandemic, racial discrimination, and hostile workplace conditions. In these respects, we who are alive today have inherited a much safer world. But, there is still much darkness to dispel.

Ironically, much of today's darkness co-exists with what appears to be light. We have more information than at any time in human history, yet, it may be harder than ever to distinguish truth from fantasy. Our modern technologies enable the past to be re-invented as never before. Computer software can place one person's head onto another person's body, in a photograph or video. Someone else's voice or words can come from another person's mouth. People can appear in scenes they never visited. Technology helps think tanks, virtual universities, and corporations to generate their own experts, with their own facts, and their own evidence, in time to publish their own books and defend just about any theory, if the price is right. Partisans and propagandists use text books to convince tomorrow's students that American slavery was not the heinous crime against humanity that it was.

Against this backdrop, we contributors feel an urgency to provide the facts as best we remember them. We are in our sixties, seventies, eighties, and one is in her nineties. We count on you who will outlive us, to safeguard the facts from the myth-makers of our time, from those technologies that recreate the past and omit our contributions.

Whether you are connected to our Ebenezer, to other churches of the African Diaspora, or to other ethnic, immigrant or urban churches, our memories may disturb you or make you laugh out loud. But, most of all, we hope they will inspire you. The first two chapters set our stories in the first half of the 20th century, in Harlem, greater New York, and the United States as a whole. Chapter three examines the spiritual context in which our founders emerged, against great odds. Our individual memories of the church and its members are catalogued in chapter four. If you pass this information to your children, and teach your children to pass it on to their children, you will be following the biblical formula — to teach truth to following generations, at every opportunity, in every format, walking along the way, sitting at home, talking in the public square.

Congratulations to all who commemorate the one hundredth anniversary of the founding of Ebenezer, a linchpin of so many lives. Your interest affirms the value in honoring those on whose shoulders we stand.

Besides the buildings they purchased, in Harlem and Brooklyn, we don't know of any physical monuments that Ebenezer's founders left behind. And monuments can be destroyed or credited to others. But, in choosing to name itself after a biblical monument, *Ebenezer*, Stone of Help, the church was teaching the value of remembering where you've come from and how God helped you get here. Over time, as their spiritual offspring spread across the city, the nation, and the globe, they carried their unique heritage, often to leadership positions in a variety of religious and secular institutions. Today, Ebenezer's legacy is not so much in stone, but in lives transformed by the faith taught and modeled there, and in communities that benefit from those lives.

***

As churches founded in the early 1900s enter their second century, they may find themselves with a smaller footprint, in neighborhoods with different demographics. Some intellectuals challenge them, arguing that the black church is dead. Certainly, many of these churches have not maintained the kind of growth and impact they had in their early years. Ebenezer's 50th anniversary souvenir journal reveals a waning Harlem congregation. By 1961, most of the first generation had moved on, to live in different communities, to worship in different churches, to reap the fruits of high-quality public education and immigrant attention to schooling and success.

During the second fifty years, new immigrant families came to Ebenezer. A younger generation took leadership, that had come of age in the Civil Rights Movement. They lit their candle for social justice, through community outreach, and alliances with other church and para-church ministries. Hopefully, the stories of that period are being written, as more perspective is gained.

Perhaps this retrospective on the first fifty years has some answers, for those who seek to reverse decline and bring about renewed spiritual impact in the community. What has surely not declined is God's power to transform lives in every era. As we consider the odds that the founders of our church faced and overcame, with God's help, we erect another stone of help, documenting for future generations what we have witnessed.

Marilyn C. Maye, Ed. D.
Editor

Contributors

In chronological order of birth, the following are those who are alive at the time of Ebenezer's centennial anniversary, who attended the church during its first fifty years, and who have written for this volume [see Part 2]:

Olwen Allman Gillman, Charlotte, North Carolina

Dorothy Greenidge Oliver, Philadelphia, Pennsylvania

Edith Farnum Rock, Brooklyn, New York

Gloria Wheatley Johnson, Princeton, New Jersey

Waldo Waterman, Harlem, New York

Hon. Carl O. Callender, Brooklyn, New York

Dr. Clive O. Callender, Silver Springs, Maryland

Luther B. Allman, Los Angeles, California

Dr. Grace Allman Burke, Dallas, Texas

Rev. Gloria W. Nurse, Washington, DC

Dr. Marilyn Allman Maye, Bronx, New York

Roxanne Johnson Kent, Montclair, New Jersey

PART 1

The American Context

The 1900s

In 1909, when the early founders of the church we celebrate began to meet in the home of Bro. William Green, America was beginning a new century. It was a time of great upheaval and of promise.

The first automobiles were on the road. Henry Ford released his Model T in 1908, becoming so popular that state governments had to register them. At the turn of the century, only vanity license plates, with their owners' initials on them, optionally ornamented the vehicles of trendy New Yorkers.[1]

On December 17, 1903, brothers Wilbur and Orville Wright, credited with inventing the first successful airplane, made four short flights at Kitty Hawk, North Carolina, with a powered glider.

But, 1909 was also the year the National Association for the Advancement of Colored People (NAACP) was organized in New York City. The NAACP was a desperate attempt by people like W.E.B. DuBois, Ida Wells-Barnett, and fair-minded whites to stop a rising tide of racist backlash against the former slaves in the southern states. The heady days of invention and industrial progress were dimmed by the rise of domestic terrorists like the Ku Klux Klan, and the legalization of inequality, ranging from the 1896 Supreme Court decision making segregation legal (Plessy v. Ferguson), to Jim Crow laws establishing a rigid caste system, with blacks at the bottom. Black Americans, by the tens of thousands, found themselves fleeing for their lives, to the Northeast, Midwest, and West coast, in the first of two Great Migrations away from the South.[2]

1910s

The founding members of Ebenezer Gospel Tabernacle were immigrants from the Caribbean. In the 1900s, they lived in midtown

Manhattan in neighborhoods with blacks from the United States. They later moved to Harlem. Some of the Caribbean blacks settled in Brooklyn, where a branch of the Christian Mission church was soon opened. These were working-class people for the most part, laboring in restaurants, on the docks, and in the homes of the emerging middle- class descendants of European immigrants. Working conditions were generally difficult, low-paid, and with little social status. It is not known how many, if any, blacks were able to find employment in factories. Many factory jobs were held by European immigrants, working under very dangerous conditions and in low-paid positions.

On March 25, 1911, a fatal fire destroyed a New York City sweatshop, the Triangle Shirtwaist Company killing nearly 150 employees, and launching major national changes in working conditions.[3] The disaster led to the creation of health and safety legislation, including factory fire codes and child-labor laws, and helped shape future labor laws.

The story of the first black policeman in New York City, appointed in 1911, sheds light on the community where Ebenezer would eventually makes its home.

"Samuel J. Battle ... was the first African-American patrolman in New York City. He joined the force in 1911, assigned first to San Juan Hill, the neighborhood where Lincoln Center is today, which preceded Harlem as one of the key African-American neighborhoods in Manhattan. He was soon moved to Harlem, as the African-American population there grew. He would later become the first African-American police sergeant (1926), lieutenant (1935), and the first African-American parole commissioner (1941)."[4]

In Ebenezer's formative days, most of the men were probably too old to be drafted to serve in World War I, although many Caribbean young people had volunteered to serve in the war as British subjects. Despite their poverty and lack of resources, God seems to have miraculously protected them during the 1918 flu pandemic.

The war had created numerous job opportunities in northern and midwestern cities, encouraging blacks from the South to migrate by the tens of thousands, escaping Jim Crow injustice. When they arrived in northern cities, many of them started branches of the churches and businesses that they had left at home. At the same time, so many Caribbean immigrants were also able to come to New York, that churches like Ebenezer could serve as havens for them, rather than be forced to make the adjustments that may have been required to unite with congregations from the Southern migrations.

1920s

As the war ended, there was a reawakening of culture and hope around the country, and Harlem was no exception. The Harlem Renaissance was a time of exuberance. Black musical culture included jazz and other popular forms, but, blacks of all backgrounds participated in a variety of sacred music traditions, including Negro spirituals, classical European music, and anthems. Music students from the historically black colleges appeared in Harlem churches singing in their classic style.

Ebenezer became well-known for its own musical performances. In the early days, it had an orchestra of musicians from a wide area and they performed at the Harlem YMCA as well as gave concerts at the church, a strong musical tradition that lasted for several decades.

For a while, the government prohibited the manufacture and sale of alcoholic beverages, giving a boost to organized crime as the sale of liquor went underground. Churches like Ebenezer, who identified with what became known as the Holiness Movement, took a strong stance against drunkenness, advocating that their members abstain completely from drinking alcoholic beverages. Drinking, smoking, social dancing, carousing, and other features of this era, were forbidden to Christians in the holiness traditions.

It was not until 1920 that the women's movement in the United States finally succeeded in getting women the right to vote.

The Immigration Act of 1924 radically reduced the number of nonwhite immigrants and those from southern and eastern Europe. Penicillin had not yet been discovered. It would be 1928 before that important discovery would provide better health care for all. Meanwhile, Bible-believing Christians relied on faith healing to do much of what home remedies and medical science at that time could not.

1930s and 1940s

Ebenezer would continue to grow and thrive despite the Great Depression, when most members were without jobs, and had to survive by all types of entrepreneurial efforts. During this decade, Hitler and the Nazis took power in Germany; and, in 1941 the Japanese attacked Pearl Harbor, prompting America to join World War 2.

Some of the children of the church members served in the war. Most of the older members had no tradition of serving in the

United States military. A second Great Migration of blacks from the South during the second world war brought hundreds of thousands more to the cities, seeking jobs that became available in the wartime economy.

After the war ended, a new period of optimism, emerged. The United Nations was formed.

1950s

In the fifties, color television was invented. A vaccine was invented to cure polio. The space race began in response to the Cold War. The Brown v. Board of Education case outlawed legal segregation in the United States.

On December 1, 1955, Rosa Parks refused to give up her seat on a Montgomery, Alabama, bus. Her arrest resulted in a boycott that lasted a year and ended with the Supreme Court declaring the segregated seating unconstitutional. This ignited the Civil Rights Movement.

1960s

By 1960, the laws limiting immigrants of color from entering the United States had diminished the stream of families coming from the Caribbean. There were fewer Christians with holiness church backgrounds seeking to worship as they had back home. A tradition of street evangelism had won some new converts in the urban areas, but, the numbers failed to make up for the shortage of new immigrants. As the civil rights laws took effect, the children of Ebenezer's founders moved to the suburbs and to other parts of the country. There were still many areas in New York where blacks faced hostility when they tried to rent or buy. But, increasingly, white flight was making it possible for black families to move away from Harlem and Brooklyn, and into the suburbs.

As Ebenezer reached its fiftieth golden anniversary, church attendance was in decline, compared to its heyday in the 1920s, 30s and 40s. In the country as a whole, a new era of unrest was being launched. President John F. Kennedy would be assassinated. The civil rights struggle was fully underway. Dr. King would preach his "I Have a Dream" speech at the 1963 March on Washington, and a few years later he would be assassinated by a gunman's bullet. New York City would experience the great blackout of 1965 and America's involvement in the Vietnam War would galvanize protests around the city and the nation.

The Caribbean Immigrant Context

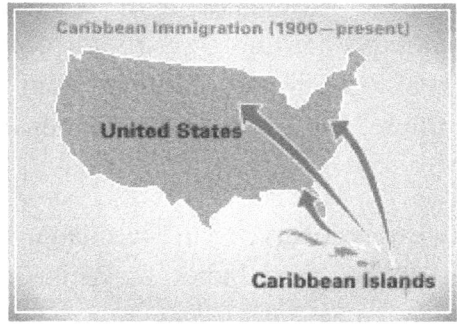

The story of the Ebenezer Gospel Tabernacle cannot be understood without some insight into the experience of being a Caribbean immigrant, or the children of Caribbean immigrants, in New York City in the first half of the 20th century.

The individuals who started Ebenezer were mostly from Barbados, one of the Caribbean islands from which blacks had been emigrating, entering the United States since the early1600s. Of course, in the 17th and 18th centuries, most of them came to the United States as slaves, rather than as immigrants. But, by the1830s, slavery had been abolished in the Caribbean, and blacks started to come to the United States as free persons. White American missionaries, inspired by the revivals of the Holiness Movement in the United States, traveled throughout the Caribbean, making converts to a revitalized form of Protestantism. Their worship was different from the ritual-bound practices of the Church of England that dominated the English-speaking islands.

In 1890, one missionary, John Hartmann, helped form The Christian Mission of the West Indies in Barbados,[5] to retain the many converts won, often by street meetings, in the revivals throughout the island. We will explore the religious context of the Christian Mission members who migrated to the United States, in the next chapter, but the political and sociological context is important to understand as well.

Before the Civil War

Before the American Civil War, the population of foreign-born blacks in the country was a little over 4,000, according to historical records.[6] Drawing from renowned black historians such as Carter G. Woodson, contemporary researchers have gleaned this roster of Caribbean blacks who became famous in pre-Civil War American black history:

Denmark Vesey (c.1767-1822) in 1822 organized in Charleston, South Carolina, what one authority accurately described as the most elaborate insurrectionary project ever formed by American slaves... Vesey was from the Virgin Islands.

John B. Russwurm (1799-1851) of Jamaica, one of the early New World settlers of Liberia, was also one of the first three black people to graduate from an American college, Bowdoin College, in Maine, in 1826.

Robert Campbell (1827-84), another Jamaican, left the island for Central America in 1852, then moved to New York in 1853. By 1855 he had become assistant principal of Philadelphia's Institute for Colored Youth. He served with distinction and was respected and admired by his colleagues and students. But exasperated by the racism he encountered in the United States, he resigned his post in 1858 to join Martin Delany in a two- man Niger Valley Exploring Party. Frustrated in his attempts to raise funds and attract Afro- American settlers for Africa, with the new hope that came with the outbreak of the Civil War, Delany abandoned his African dream and became an officer in the Union Army.

Jan Earnst Matzeliger (1852-89), the inventor of a revolutionary; shoe-making machine, had migrated from Suriname.[7]

The 1860s and beyond

After the Civil War, the numbers of "foreign-born" blacks had increased to over 20,000. Among them were the following:

Joseph Sandiford Atwell, a Barbadian, in 1867 became the first black man after the Civil War to be ordained in the Episcopal Church in the United States.

Bert Williams (1875-1922), the famous comedian, was born in Antigua... [8]

These 19th century Caribbean immigrants to America gave birth to children, many of whom distinguished themselves intellectually, culturally, and politically. Some of them were:

W. E. B. Du Bois (1868-1963),

James Weldon Johnson (1871-1938), his brother Rosamond Johnson (1873-1954),

William Stanley Braithwaite (1878-1962),

James Weldon Johnson

Grace Campbell (1882-1943)[9]

The Twentieth Century

In the twentieth century, numerous autobiographies have helped historians understand the nature and impact of black immigration from the Caribbean to the United States. Here are some of them:

<u>Autobiographies by those born or raised in the Caribbean</u>

Carmichael, Stokely, with Ekwueme Michael Thelwell. *Ready for Revolution: The Life and*

Struggles of Stokely Carmichael (Kwame Toure). New York: Scribner, 2003.

Chisholm, Shirley. *Unbought and Unbossed.* Boston: Houghton Mifflin Co., 1970.

Ferguson, Ira Lunan. *I Dug Graves at Night to Attend College by Day: An Autobiography,* vol. 1, New York: Theo. Gaus' Sons, 1968; vols. 2 and 3, San Francisco: The Lunan-Ferguson Library, 1969, 1970.

Jack, Hulan. *Fifty Years A Democrat: The Autobiography of Hulan Jack.* New York: New Benjamin Franklin House, 1980.

McKay, Claude. *A Long Way From Home.* New York: Lee Furman, 1937.

Makonnen, Ras, as recorded and edited by Kenneth King. *Pan-Africanism from Within.* Nairobi: Oxford University Press, 1973.

Mulzac, Hugh, as told to Louis Burnham and Norval Welch. *A Star to Steer By.* New York: International Publishers, 1963.

Poitier, Sidney. *This Life.* New York: Alfred A. Knopf, 1980.

———. *The Measure of a Man: A Spiritual Autobiography.* San Francisco: Harper San Francisco, 2000.

Somerville, J. Alexander. *Man of Colour: An Autobiography.* Los Angeles: Lorrin L. Morrison, 1949.

Staupers, Mabel Keaton. *No Time for Prejudice: A Story of the Integration of Negroes in Nursing in the United States.* New York: Macmillan, 1961.

Walter, John C. *The Harlem Fox J. Raymond Jones and Tammany,* 1920–1970. Albany: State University of New York Press, 1989.

Williams, Eric. *Inward Hunger: The Education of a Prime Minister.* London: Andre Deutsch, 1969.

Autobiographies by those of Caribbean parentage

Guinier, Lani. *Lift Every Voice: Turning a Civil Rights Setback Into a New Vision of Social Justice.* New York: Simon and Schuster, 1998.

Johnson, James Weldon. *Along This Way.* 1933, reprint, New York: Penguin Books, 1990.

Lorde, Audre. *Zami: A New Spelling of My Name.* 1982, reprint. Freedom, Calif.: The Crossing Press, 1994.

Motley, Constance Baker. *Equal Justice under Law: An Autobiography.* New York: Farrar, Straus and Giroux, 1998.

Powell, Colin, with Joseph Persico. *My American Journey.* New York: Random House, 1995.

X, Malcolm, with the assistance of Alex Haley. *The Autobiography of Malcolm X.* New York: Grove Press, 1965.

The large number of autobiographies reflects the high rates of literacy among these immigrants. In fact, one historian notes that blacks from the Caribbean were more literate than the average white American before the 1960s.[10] The overwhelming majority of them settled in New York City, during this period, with Florida and Massachusetts following in second and third place for the size of their Caribbean immigrant populations. Throughout the period, black women immigrants consistently outnumbered men.

> "It has been estimated that, by the 1930s, a third of New York's black professionals, including doctors, dentists and lawyers, came from the ranks of Caribbean migrants—a figure well in excess of the group's size within the city's black population. Furthermore, the Caribbean newcomers accounted for a disproportionately large number of black businessmen and -women in New York City. A study of the entries in *Who's Who in Colored America,* the most comprehensive guide to Afro-America's elite at the time, covering the period from 1915 to 1932, yielded a disproportionately high presence of black migrants. In 1930 only 0.8 percent of the black population of America was of foreign birth. Yet 6 percent of those listed were migrants. Over 8 percent of the doctors, 4.5 percent of the lawyers, more than 14 percent of the businessmen, 4.5 percent of the clergymen, over 3 percent of the professors, and 4 percent of the writers/authors listed for the period were migrants. No doubt the proportion would have been higher if the data included those of immigrant

descent instead of being confined to those of foreign birth.

"Among the sons and daughters of this first generation of Caribbean migrants is a phalanx of distinguished Afro-Americans: Malcolm X, Louis Farrakhan, Harry Belafonte, Colin Powell, St. Clair Drake, Clifford Alexander, Bruce Llewelyn, Cicely Tyson, Maida Springer Kemp, Vincent Harding, Robert Moses, Shirley Chisholm, Constance Baker Motley, Mamie Phipps Clark, Margaret Walker, Kareem Abdul-Jabbar, Audre Lorde, Michelle Wallace, Paule Marshall, Yaphet Kotto, Sonny Rollins, Rosa Guy, June Jordan, and Lani Guinier."[11]

The congregations of the holiness churches, whether African-American or Caribbean in origin, were not particularly known to include blacks prominent in public life, such as those listed above. Black public figures generally frequented churches with "high church," or more liturgical traditions, where they would have contact with others of their social standing. Reading through the society pages of the local newspapers at that time, you are more likely to find weddings, funerals, and other events involving black celebrities having taken place at the Episcopal or Presbyterian churches. By contrast, those in the holiness churches were guarded about too close association with wealth and fame. They wanted to be careful to heed the scriptural warning against "gaining the world and losing one's soul."[12] It would have been difficult to remain in such churches and aspire to become an actor, an entertainer, or other occupations associated with "carnal" lifestyles.

African-American Migration from the South

Today we have the research of journalist Isabel Wilkerson (2010), in her ground-breaking work, *The Warmth of Other Suns*, for historical information about the 6 million sons and daughters of the First and Second Great Migrations from the South to the North, beginning around the same time that Ebenezer was formed. Although a majority of those from the southern states migrated to other cities, such as Chicago, Cleveland, Detroit, Los Angeles, and Philadelphia, New York's population was also greatly enlarged and was enriched by these migrants, as well. The Great Migrations were spurred by the rise of the Ku Klux Klan, Jim Crow laws, natural disasters, and by employment opportunities in the North, as the flow of European immigration narrowed with the outbreak of World War 1. Wilkerson reports census data showing that black migrants from the South were better educated, worked more jobs, and had more stable family lives than the northern-born blacks and whites in many of the communities to which they fled.[13]

Historian James Gregory (2005) argues that the out-migration from the South, dubbed the Southern Diaspora, brought the religious culture of the South, Pentecostalism, for example, to the North, and helped build a powerful black base that would be vital for supporting the Civil Rights Movement.[14]

Among the many sons and daughters of these Great Migrations were the following:

Zora Neale Hurston (1891 – 1960) who left Alabama to go to Howard University, and then to Barnard College in New York City, in the middle of the Harlem Renaissance. She became an anthropologist, a journalist and an author, who received full recognition only after her death.

Other famous African-Americans included Paul Robeson (1989 – 1976), scholar, activist, opera singer, athlete, only the third black to attend Rutgers University, and a graduate of Columbia University Law School, was the son of a slave who had escaped to the North before the Great Migrations, and who raised his family in New Jersey, after serving in the Civil War for the Union Army. His brother was a pastor in the AME Zion Church in New York City, the first black church in New York State.[15]

Percy Sutton (1920 – 2009) was a lawyer, politician, businessman, who served as state assemblyman, President of the Borough of Manhattan, and ran unsuccessfully for mayor of New York City. The son of educators and entrepreneurs, he migrated north from San Antonio, Texas to go to law school at Brooklyn Law School, and defended Malcolm X and others. His business investments in the New York Amsterdam News, the Apollo Theatre, and the Inner City Broadcasting Network, together with his mentoring of local politicians like David Dinkins and David Patterson, made him an icon in New York's black community.[16]

Evangelist Tom Skinner (1942 – 1994) talks about his parents leaving Greenville, South Carolina for Harlem during the Great Migration, in an interview in the Billy Graham archives at Wheaton College. [17] A leader in the Harlem Evangelistic Association, in 1962, he became famous for preaching Billy Graham-style evangelistic meetings at Harlem's Apollo Theater. The son of a preacher, and a voracious reader and social critic himself since childhood, Tom Skinner developed into a powerful orator and proclaimer of the gospel message, with a passion for social justice. He inspired a generation of pastors, who still serve today, with his messages, books, broadcasts, and a leadership institute that he launched in the Washington, DC area.

Actors and film producers Denzel Washington and Spike Lee are contemporary sons of the Great Migrations North.[18]

Great Black Churches Forged from Two In- Migrations

A look at Ebenezer's neighboring churches along Lenox Avenue provides insight into the challenges of assimilation that faced blacks from these two migrations:

- Ephesus Seventh Day Adventist Church, at 123rd Street
- St. Martin Episcopal Church, at 122nd Street
- Mt. Morris Park Presbyterian Church, was on 121st and Mount Morris Park, one block east
- Mount Olivet Baptist Church, at 120th Street
- Literally next door to Ebenezer, the Congregational Church of God, at 121st Street.

It is likely that the members of the first two of these churches were predominantly from the Caribbean in-migration,[19] and the members of the last three, were predominantly from the South-to-North migration. In their heyday, all of these churches were bustling, thriving congregations, with attendance well into the hundreds on their worship days. The Church of God next door to Ebenezer was smaller; their sanctuary was in a retro-fitted residential building; and, their congregation probably was a little over 100.

A look at the National Church of God website today confirms the historical trends noted here:

> "The National Association of the Church of God was officially organized in 1916... From its earliest existence, without knowing that a doctrinally similar "reformation" had begun in western Michigan, it has been an independent autonomous organization that envisioned the uniting of African-American "immigrants" who were migrating from the South in search of new beginnings and new opportunities. Incredible growth occurred with the influx of men and women from the South and Mid-Atlantic areas.
>
> In 1917, [it] changed its name to the National Association of the Church of God. Many of the new southern constituency brought information regarding a wonderful movement called the Reformation Movement of the Church of God headquartered in Anderson, Indiana. Soon after its incorporation, influenced by many ministers migrating to it from the South, the National Association began to affiliate with the Church of God, Anderson.
>
> Today, the National Association of the Church of God is an organization of over 420 churches ... with headquarter offices located in [20]West Middlesex, Pennsylvania.
>
> The National Association seeks to be a community that assists and involves all persons regardless of age, ethnic background, creed, educational level, or economic status."[21]

This diplomatic explanation of the black church's history delicately sidesteps the fact that the Church of God in Anderson, Indiana remained predominantly the white version of the Church of God, and a look at their websites confirms that the groups have pretty much remained separate, although both profess to be integrated today. Ebenezer's next-door neighbor through most of its early years on Lenox Avenue was from the Church of God, of the black, southern migration. Before they relocated to Amsterdam Avenue in the 1970s, the two pastors and congregations visited each other's church on special occasions, such as each church's anniversary.

It is my recollection, supported by articles in the archives of the local newspaper[22], that there was great respect for each other among the Harlem churches' clergy, and that there was professional contact among them. A source of collaboration was the New York Bible Society. The Society had an African-American representative, Dr. V. Simpson Turner[23], who, during the 1950s, organized outreach programs in the black churches around the city. One of those programs was an annual Bible quiz competition, designed to promote knowledge and study of the scriptures. Sponsored by the Bible society, quizzes were aired on radio station WWRL, at the end of the AM dial, that targeted the black listening audience. A variety of competitions throughout the year culminated in a final competition that was often held at Ephesus Seventh Day Adventist Church, who had a sanctuary large enough to house the hundreds of congregants from the various churches who would attend to support their quizzing teams.[24] A photograph of teams from Ebenezer and Ephesus, competing in a Bible quiz on air, appeared in the New York Amsterdam News February 2, 1957 edition.[25]

In hindsight, these quizzing programs built opportunities, not only for intellectual and spiritual development among the participating congregations, but also for unity across denominational and cultural lines. Given the strong holiness tradition of the Ebenezer congregation, it is not surprising that our church was highly represented among contest winners each year. In our tradition, weekly Bible study, weekly opportunities to state testimonies about our personal faith, and emphasis on biblical knowledge and application put us at an advantage over those who participated from church traditions whose lay members had less opportunity for Bible study and public expression of their faith.

The Challenge of Assimilation

The relationship between the black Caribbean immigrants and the American-born descendants of African slaves, many of whom were also migrants to the Northern states, is often discussed informally or depicted in literature, but little studied with academic rigor. This writer was so intrigued by the topic as a college student in the late 1960s, I wrote an extensively researched paper on the subject, using the resources of the Schomburg Center for Research. I pored over books, journals, newspaper and magazine articles, letters and sermon notes, to get a sense of the thoughts and feelings of blacks who lived in the period when the people of both migrations came together.

Obituaries and burial records of those from this era provide insights into these great migrations. In the archives of Harlem's *New York Amsterdam News*, you can often tell by the undertaker's name which migration the deceased was from. For example, directly opposite Ebenezer on Lenox Avenue were two prominent funeral homes, a few doorsteps apart: The Mickey Funeral Home and the Henry A. Toppin Funeral Home. Clients of the Mickey Funeral Home (aka The Carolina Chapel) were predominantly from the south, such as from Charleston, South Carolina where it was founded.[26] Mr. Toppin, a Barbadian, served an overwhelmingly Caribbean clientele. While different black families sought out morticians of their same cultural roots, if they didn't send home the bodies of their loved ones, they generally buried them at the same places in New York. According to the records of Woodlawn Cemetery, preserved in association with Columbia University, "at the close of the 19th century, Woodlawn...emerged as the chosen burial ground for New Yorkers of African American and Afro Caribbean descent."[27]

Although their parents made limited efforts to assimilate, the children of the immigrants couldn't assimilate fast enough. The memoirs in a later chapter reflect a lot of the humor that the first generation found in their parents' accents and quirky food and fashion preferences. The dominant accent in the black community at that time were the accents of the southern states, as waves of black migrants from the coastal states of Florida, Georgia, North and South Carolina, and Virginia settled in Harlem and Brooklyn.

Although the children of black immigrants may never have visited the South, they could sport a mean southern accent, and, today, many in their eighties still speak as though they grew up in the southern states, although they may never have even visited there. To speak in even a "standard" American accent, was to invite the dreaded question, "Where are your people from?" and to risk feeling like an outsider among one's peers at school, or work, or in the neighborhood. Unlike Caribbean immigrants of the later immigration periods (after the 1970s), who proudly speak their patois and whose reggae and calypso music have strong mainstream appeal, the children of the earlier migrations pretty much kept their background under wraps, and tried to blend in as much as possible.

To be fair, we should note that neither the migrants from the south nor those from the Caribbean were uniform in their worship associations. Different churches tended to have majorities from specific islands, countries, or American states. Some churches were distinctly Carolinian. When Barbadians and Jamaicans migrated to Panama to work on building the Panama Canal at the turn of the 20th century, many of them took their religious beliefs, gave their children Spanish names, and learned to speak Spanish. Many remain there to this day, members of the Christian Mission of Panama. Those that migrated on to New York brought a uniquely Panamanian sensibility that distinguished them from other immigrants who had come directly from the Caribbean. Although they have a common foundation and identical creeds, they remained a church organization separate from the Christian Mission of USA, with their own congregations in Harlem and Brooklyn.[28]

Special musical events, such as performances of spirituals and classics by student choirs from Historically Black Colleges travelling in the tradition of the Fisk Jubilee singers, provided rare opportunities for churchgoers from both migrations to engage and to develop appreciation for each other. The Bible Society sponsored unifying events, such as "Universal Bible Sunday" and special interchurch Bible study programs.[29]

But, such occasional, cooperative programs did not, in general, achieve on-going fellowship and worship among blacks of the two migrations. Some denominations were somewhat more successful at this than were others. The Seventh-Day Adventists had what is now Oakwood University in Huntsville, Alabama, where blacks of different cultural backgrounds studied together for ministry. According to their website, it "was founded in 1896 with the purpose of providing African Americans with Christian education."[30] Such common experiences were helpful in building bridges within their church, and famous alumni, like singers Wintley Phipps and Take 6, reflect diverse Caribbean and southern roots.[31]

In *Soldiers of Uncommon Valor*, his history of blacks in the Salvation Army, Warren L. Maye[32] documents, within a holiness denomination, the struggles and successes in developing a multi-cultural witness. The pioneering work of the Army in America was launched among African-Americans in Cleveland, Ohio in the 1870s, and the church's highest ranking black clergyperson, recently retired National Commander Israel Gaither, is an African-American.[33] At the same time, however, there is a strong, possibly stronger, Caribbean presence among the organization's black rank and file. Members and leaders of Ebenezer fellowshipped with officers and soldiers of the Harlem Salvation Army Corps on special occasions, during the mid-1900s.

Congregations where the pastor and his wife came from the different migrations (there were few female senior pastors in those days) provided strong role models for cross-cultural fellowship. One such marriage was that of the late Bishop Roderick Caesar and his wife Rev. Gertrude Caesar, who co-founded the Bethel Gospel Assembly in Jamaica, New York. A Pentecostal church, that had much in common with other holiness churches, they managed to grow a strong congregation with balanced leadership and representation by blacks who were from the Caribbean and from the southern states. He was from St. Lucia, and she was from Pittsburgh, Pennsylvania. They represented an unusual partnership of strong male and female, and black cross-cultural, pastoral leadership, which is common today, but was rare in the 1950s. As can be seen in a recent tribute published by their daughter, Rev. Beverly Caesar Sherrod, the churches they founded are still thriving today.[34]

A 2010 Debate: Is the Black Church Dead?

A cautionary tale remains for congregations who are built on the more recent waves of black immigration, that occurred since the late 1960s: *Stay in cultural isolation at your own peril.* Any observer of the period from the 1950s through the 1970s will notice that most of the churches on the section of Lenox Avenue where Ebenezer stands entered decline in midlife. The influx of new immigrants had slowed to a trickle, both from the Caribbean and the southern states, too few to keep them growing, large and prosperous. Their children were not interested in remaining identified with or circumscribed by their parents' cultural heritage. As Jesus taught his disciples to leave Jerusalem and to go to Samaria and to the uttermost parts of the earth, so immigrants and migrants who profess to live out the gospel would do well to resist the temptation to cling to the familiar at the expense of reaching others who need to encounter the Christ of the gospel.

Many other factors contribute to the later decline of churches like those along that strip of Lenox Avenue, more than we can consider in this narrative. Princeton University's Professor of Religion and African-American Studies, Dr. Eddie Glaude,[35] made headlines in February 2010 by his provocative article in the Huffington Post proclaiming, *"The Black Church Is Dead."* An ensuing debate among black scholars at Columbia University's Institute for Research in African-American Studies[36] captures the concern of many that the critical role that the black church has played in the history and development of people of African descent in America, particularly in the northern, urban areas, may be coming to an end. Some of the reasons they cite are: the rise of look-alike worship in predominantly white non-denominational settings; the growth of mega-churches and prosperity ministries, some with little concern for economic justice; an extreme focus on anti-abortion and anti-gay rights to the exclusion of social justice programs for their own people; and, the tendency to live in the past, rather than to remain a prophetic voice in changing times.

It was in the black church, more than anywhere else in black culture, except perhaps on the campuses of Historically Black Colleges and Universities, that black youth were taught from an early age that, if they were successful, it was because God had a purpose for their lives, one that necessarily included the uplift of the race. The iconic biblical characters of Joseph, second in command to the Egyptian Pharaoh; of Moses, raised in a later Pharaoh's household; and of Queen Esther, made the wife of the King of Persia "for such a time as this" [37]– all laid the groundwork for developing a sense of responsibility to use one's blessings for the benefit of one's own people and for the wider community. Today, the culture of individualism has snuffed out much of this idealism. Too many young black people resent any hint that they owe their success to any but their own efforts; and they trumpet their freedom to blaze their own trails and pursue their own dreams, without feeling guilt or responsibility for the lot of less-privileged blacks. It is noteworthy that this change has occurred as the influence of the black church has weakened. Perhaps, if people gain insight into the role the black church has played in their own lives, that may be the first step in ensuring that the black church survives and thrives.

The Holiness Revival Context

In the prior chapter, we were introduced to several churches that were neighbors of Ebenezer along Lenox Avenue. Throughout Harlem, churches could be found with names that reflected the biblical journey of the Children of Israel, with whom black migrants and immigrants could readily identify. Churches with names like Mt. Moriah, Mt. Nebo, Mt. Pisgah, Shiloh, and Canaan called to memory recognized Bible locations, often with well-known events associated with them. *Ebenezer* is a less distinctive biblical landmark. Commonly adopted by black churches, it literally means, in the Hebrew language, "Stone of Help."

The biblical Ebenezer was a stone monument set up by the weary Israelites, as they battled enemies, once they arrived in the Promised Land.[38] The name is found in the book of 1 Samuel chapter 7 and verse 12, *"Then Samuel took a stone and set it up between Mizpah and Shen, and called its name Ebenezer, saying, 'Thus far the Lord has helped us'."*[39] It would be years before King Solomon built a permanent house of worship; so they had worshipped in a tabernacle, a movable tent, that God would visit in response to the prayers of his people. The "Stone of Help" was one of several markers they erected, to remind future generations of how God had helped them to that point in their history as an embattled people.

Ebenezer Gospel Tabernacle was the name we went by, although, in the early days the church was more commonly known as *"The Christian Mission of the U.S.A,"* or simply, *"The Mission."* We were not Baptist, or Presbyterian, or explicitly Methodist, names of large denominations that most people were familiar with. Although we didn't refer to ourselves as being part of a movement, the church was an outgrowth of what became known as the Holiness Movement, which had its roots in England and the Wesleyan revival, that spread to the United States and spawned a generation of white American missionaries who evangelized internationally.

Christians and their Missions

In the 1880s, white American missionaries from the Christian and Missionary Alliance denomination went to Barbados and founded a mission there, that they called the Christian Mission of the West Indies. Shortly before and again at the turn of the 20th century, several spiritual revivals had broken out around the United States.

The roots of these revivals can be traced to the ministry of the Wesley brothers, John and Charles, who had had a profound influence on Protestantism, especially on the Church of England where they had served as clergy in the middle and late 1700s. Their open-air meetings and evangelical teaching called Christians to personal holiness, Bible study and discipleship, as well as to social justice. They believed that Christians had to engage in on-going spiritual growth, striving for holiness and ultimate perfection, if they were to be sure of ultimate salvation. They created small groups to help keep people accountable. They encouraged lay persons to preach and lead, and got into trouble with the official church because of their unorthodox practices. Their movement was known as Methodism, a branch of which later evolved into the Holiness Movement.

The messages of the Wesleys were timely, as the international slave trade and the rise of industrialization had brought fortunes to a few, at the expense of the many. The stories of Charles Dickens, with characters such as Scrooge and Oliver Twist, capture some of the social tensions that developed over time. By the 1800s, the consciences of many English speakers in Britain and her current and former colonies had been pricked by movements focused on personal accountability for both themselves as well as for the poor, for prisoners, and for slaves, such as the anti-slavery work of William Wilberforce[40] and the social justice work of William Booth's Salvation Army. Revivals began to break out on both sides of the Atlantic Ocean, including one in Rhode Island in the late

1800s. American preachers like Dwight L. Moody travelled to and from New England to England preaching.

Dividing Lines

In 1905, under the leadership of an African-American holiness preacher, named William J. Seymour, Pentecostal revival broke out in the Azusa Street revival in Los Angeles that lasted for three years, night and day. It was not long before a number of new church organizations arose to give voice and embodiment to the message of sanctification and spirit fullness. In the heat of revival fervor, blacks and whites worshipped God together, in common realization of their sinfulness before a holy and just God. When revival fervor cooled, many retreated to their old cultural habits. Separate black and white congregations reflected legal and de facto segregation in the United States; white-only clergy reflected colonialism's racial and social boundaries in Africa and the Caribbean. The Christian and Missionary Alliance (CMA) was one such group in the United States.

One of the key dividing lines among the many holiness churches that emerged from these revivals was the issue of speaking in tongues as evidence of the presence of the Holy Spirit in one's life. One holiness group, now known as the Church of God (Anderson, Indiana) makes a point of this in writing their official history:

> "The Church of God, with U.S. offices in Anderson, Indiana, began in 1881 as a movement emphasizing the unity of God's people and holy living. ...This movement is not historically related to the several Church of God bodies rooted in the holiness revival of Tennessee and the Carolinas in the late nineteenth century. Although it shares their holiness commitment, it does not emphasize the charismatic

gift of speaking in tongues generally associated with Pentecostal churches.

Deeply influenced by Wesleyan theology and Pietism, the church's generally accepted teachings include the divine inspiration of Scripture; forgiveness of sin through the atonement of Jesus Christ and repentance of the believer; the experience of holiness; the personal return of Christ, unconnected with any millennial reign; the kingdom of God as established here and now; the resurrection of the dead; and a final judgment in which there will be reward for the righteous and punishment for the wicked....

In 1891, the movement's first missionary was sent to Mexico. Since those early days, the Church of God has continued to grow into a multinational community of faith. At present, the largest concentrations of U.S. churches are in the Midwest, along the Pacific Coast, and in western Pennsylvania."[41]

They point out their difference from the Church of God (Cleveland, Tennessee), which is the larger organization and the second largest Pentecostal denomination, next to the Assemblies of God. [42]

The history of the various holiness denominations today have similar trends, starting out of revival fervor, and diverting into separate movements over differences in doctrine and cultural preferences. Although the Christian Mission of the West Indies and the USA were never officially part of the Christian and Missionary Alliance (CMA), they were offshoots, separated primarily by cultural barriers. One key contact with the Christian and Missionary Alliance was with Jamaican-born Rev. Montrose Waite, who had attended Nyack Institute, as it was called in the 1920s.

> "... educated at the CMA's Nyack Institute in New York State. After suffering repeated setbacks and rebuffs in his attempts to go to Africa as a missionary because of the color of his skin, he finally sailed under CMA auspices in 1923 to Sierra Leone. He and his family returned on furlough to the United States in 1937 and were unable to return to Africa with the CMA because of opposition at the time of many CMA clergy and missionaries to black missionaries. Through many hardships and discouragement, he and his wife remained true to their calling. He eventually was able to find enough like-minded supporters to found in 1947 the Afro-American Missionary Crusade (AAMC)"[43]

Rev. Waite, his wife and seven children labored in Liberia for decades, supported by a variety of churches including Ebenezer.[44]

Later the CMA school became known as Nyack Missionary College, and now is so mainstream in the New York metropolitan area, that the word "missionary" is no longer in its name. Rev. Waite would have been one of the first blacks to attend, as the school did not accept black students until the 1920s, nearly forty years after its founding. The first African-American to work on Evangelist Billy Graham's team, Howard Jones, was one of a few black students that attended Nyack in the early years, and he and his wife's experience is documented in *Living in Two Worlds:*[45]

> "In a student body of six hundred, we were two of twelve blacks. That meant we couldn't easily blend in with the rest of the students. One of those other blacks was Ruth, a senior with whom I roomed my first year. It was 1941 and the school had welcomed

blacks only twenty years earlier, so we still felt like "test cases." The white students weren't accustomed to having blacks on campus, and since most had never associated with blacks in their churches or communities, many of them treated us rudely. We were always conscious of their watching eyes and listening ears evaluating our collective lives.

"I was disappointed to find the same old prejudices and the same old hate stares on a Christian campus. It's no wonder our little group of black students enjoyed being together whenever we could. Occasionally I'd rankle inwardly when a white male would open the door for another white student and then let it close in my face, but I was trying to overlook such rudeness. Often our group discussed the issue of prejudice within the church, but found we had no solutions. The white community expected us to know "our place" and to be docile, smiling Christians, even though the Scriptures emphasized our equality in Christ."

Schools like Nyack turned out young people, eager to serve as missionaries in foreign countries, but, who by their lifestyles and training, had little meaningful contact with or insight into the lives of people of different races. Eleven o'clock on Sunday became known as the most segregated hour in America. When the new converts came to the United States, they did not typically worship with the congregations where their missionaries had come from.

In Barbados, American missionaries conducted "open-air" services and visited rural churches and revival broke out. Numerous islanders left the Anglican Church and joined forces with these missionary ministries, which gave them more opportunity to express their faith, and to develop and use their talents. These ministries eventually became Caribbean outposts of American denominations, such as the Church of the Nazarene, the Church of the Pilgrim Holiness, the Church of God, and the Pentecostal Assemblies of God. The Christian Mission of the West Indies was founded by missionaries of the Christian and Missionary Alliance, but they did not formally affiliate with the U.S. church denomination, choosing a similar name, and maintaining a strong evangelistic and missions focus.

Holiness Traditions

A very strict code of life and conduct was observed by these converts, as the movement gave top priority to personal piety. My father's parents, Charles Allman and Clara Cox Allman, who never had the opportunity to visit the United States, were typical Barbadian converts. They drastically changed their own lifestyles, in response to revival and biblical teaching, as well as their demands on their children, my father and his siblings. Although we typically associate abstaining from pork with the Seventh Day Adventists, my father never ate it, as a matter of conscience, although he did not require his family to do so. Holiness groups were known for austere dress and for refraining from worldly pleasures, such as drinking alcoholic beverages, smoking tobacco products, gambling, and carousing. All members were supposed to engage in vigorous evangelization through public meetings, evenings and weekends, in the perennially warm weather. Hand-clapping and tambourine beating were common components of worship. In every service, there was a call to pray at an altar, for persons to demonstrate their commitment to worshipping God in the ways made popular by these fast-growing religious groups.[46]

When persons who had become converted into the holiness denominations came to the United States, they naturally looked to join groups who practiced their particular brand of Protestantism. It was not long before they realized they were not welcome in the mainstream of the denominations which their missionary mentors had come from. Rather than turn back from their faith, they turned to build their own organizations. The combination of vigorous immigration and religious proselytizing made these churches numerous in the early days of the 1900s.

***

It is in this context that a group began meeting at the home of a Brother William Green, in 1909, and within a decade had four churches around Manhattan and Brooklyn. These were incorporated in the State of the New York as an independent denomination, no longer part of the Christian Mission of the West Indies. With plenty of recruits coming off the boats at Ellis Island every year, there was little need to join forces with the African-American holiness groups, such as the Church of God (Anderson), the Church of God In Christ, and the Fire Baptized Holiness churches, and some Baptist churches, and to adopt their unique style of music and worship. To the extent that white American holiness groups were slow to welcome blacks of either American or Caribbean background into their worship, their congregations remained largely racially separate.

Occasionally, missionaries who had lived abroad and were comfortable worshipping with people of color, relocated to black holiness churches in the United States, and helped the congregations with administrative and other practical needs. This practice continued well into the 1940s and 1950s. The writer recalls being a young child in Daily Vacation Bible School at Ebenezer, and being taught by a white missionary, who came to Harlem every summer, for that purpose. She played the piano, taught us songs from the U.S. heartland, and helped us make arts and crafts. Unfortunately, there was little cross-cultural in the production of Christian Education materials and there were no black characters depicted with which the children could identify. It wasn't long before the children found the missionary offerings out-of-date and unappealing.

It was one such missionary, Sister Annie Coope, who helped the fledgling branch of the Christian Mission of the West Indies, that had been meeting in homes in Manhattan since 1909, to find and "call" their first pastor. She suggested someone who had been converted in the Barbados Christian Mission, but lived at the time in the United States. He was Rev. Eustace Farnum, who before moving to Rhode Island, had served for a while as a missionary to South America. He accepted the call to move with his wife and children to New York, and to pastor the new work. Beginning in 1911, he led the expansion to four churches, in Manhattan and Brooklyn. The purpose of the new church organization was stated as: "the promotion of domestic and foreign missions, and the preaching of the Gospel wherever a Door of Service is open to us." As the church grew, they elected Elder Farnum as General Superintendent and incorporated the church as the Christian Mission of the U.S.A, no longer formally affiliated with the Barbados Mission. Elder Farnum was assisted and mentored for over thirty years by American missionary, John Hartman, who had founded the Mission in the West Indies. Elder Hartman served as Assistant Superintendent in the New York mission.

The specifics of the church's history during its first fifty years are contained in other documents, including the *50th Anniversary Journal*, produced in 1961. A list of some of the active members during that period, who are now deceased appears in the Legacies section at the back of this book. Although this volume focuses on the Harlem branch of Ebenezer, which also served as headquarters during this period, the church in Brooklyn reflects and has contributed to the rich history of black people from both migrations. A list of some of the Brooklyn stalwarts appears in the Legacies section as well, including Rev. George Simpson, who was Assistant Pastor in Brooklyn, during most of Elder Farnum's pastorate of all the churches. Rev. Simpson became pastor in

Brooklyn, and Rev. Luther Allman in Harlem, when Pastor Farnum retired from the pastorate in 1950.[47]

    The fruits of the ministry of Ebenezer are many and far-reaching. Although most of the pioneers never sat in a college classroom, and many never even attended high school, they educated themselves by studying the Scriptures and by taking advantage of available opportunities for development. As a result, they nurtured generations of pastors and missionaries, doctors and nurses, lawyers and judges, educators and authors, musicians and actors, entrepreneurs and public servants, and others whom we may never know about. Some of those who knew the founders and are still alive to celebrate Ebenezer's centennial anniversary have written memoirs that appear in Part 2. Their memories, as well as their own accomplishments, offer insights into the impact of this relatively inconspicuous congregation. Readers who trace their roots to similar churches will likely find much that is familiar. Whatever your background, in these stories you can see that the Helper behind the name Ebenezer has surely proven worthy of their trust.

PART 2

Memoirs

Olwen Allman Gillman, born in the 1910s

".. All my children (4) were christened at Ebenezer"

The oldest person we could find alive today, at the time of this writing, who knew the founders of the Christian Mission is Mrs. Olwen Allman Gillman, now a resident of Charlotte, North Carolina. As a youngster, Olwen Gillman is pictured in the back of this book with the Sunday school students on the steps of 15 West 127th Street, one of Ebenezer's early locations. Later a beautician and homemaker, like many of the children of "The Mission", she associates the church with all of the major milestones in her life.

***

Ebenezer gave me a real loving childhood through several Sunday school teachers who taught me the religious aspects of giving my heart to the Lord, at an early age.

As I grew, I attended Tuesday evening's Youth Ministry. I continued attending Ebenezer even when they moved from 127th Street to 121st Street and Lenox Avenue. I worshiped with my parents and got married, through Ebenezer, at Mt. Moriah Baptist Church.

All my children (4) were christened at Ebenezer. I continued taking my parents there when they became aged and were no longer able to drive themselves. When they passed on to their just rewards, they were funeralized at Ebenezer. After their deaths, I joined another church with my husband, and am still a member of that church although I have moved to another state.

Ebenezer taught me to love God, serve and honor Him which I am still doing at my tender age of 92.

Dorothy Greenidge Oliver, born in the 1920s

"....I began playing the piano for Sunday services when I was in Junior High, about 12-13 years old... Ebenezer services were very lively...."

Dorothy Oliver spent many years in India, serving as a missionary, along with her husband and children. Her memories of Ebenezer go back to her childhood.

***

My earliest memory of Ebenezer Christian Mission is riding as a child in the outside rumble seat of Rev. Farnum's car with Florence Brown.

The original church was located at 15 W. 127th Street, between Lenox Avenue and 5th Avenue. My home was at 31 W. 127th Street, in the same block.

I would attend Children's Meeting on Tuesday evenings. It was there that I accepted the Lord as my Savior. I was around 9 or 10 years old. The only friends I remember were Lenora and Gloria Wheatley, who lived across the street from us and their cousin, Florence Brown; we played often together.

Every year we would attend the Church picnic. Sometimes we would ride up the Hudson River by boat, and sometimes by bus. It was a lot of fun for us young people. Often we'd sing while traveling on the boat. Sometimes our picnics would include members of our sister church, Ebenezer Christian Mission in Brooklyn.

I began playing the piano for Sunday services when I was in Junior High, about 12-13 years old, after my sister Ruth, who had been the pianist, married. Ebenezer services were very lively. Bro. Wheatley would play his guitar while I played the piano.

I played for Ebenezer services until I married my husband, Rev. H. Douglas Oliver, at Ebenezer, at its new location on Lenox Avenue. We then relocated to Birmingham, Alabama.

Edith Farnum Rock, born in the 1920s

"...In addition to Bible study, he taught music, art and even sports...."

Edith Rock served as a public health nurse in Newark, Washington, DC and Brooklyn, New York. She also taught health education and innovated a sex education curriculum, in a university nursing program. Now retired, she still has vivid memories of her grandfather, the original pastor of Ebenezer.

***

I remember my grandfather, Reverend Ethelbert Eustace Farnum,... a bold stately figure dressed in black from head to toe, dominating everything in view.... I always felt intimidated by his grandeur. Today, in 2011, as his 87-year old granddaughter, I offer some hazy memories him.

Early Childhood Memories

I am about four years old. The setting is a church assembly. There are joyous sounds of singing and tambourines. Grandfather is standing at a lectern, with a rod in his hand directed toward a canvas scroll with painted biblical scenes. Congregants are seated on wooden folding chairs. My mother appears attentive and happy. My brother, Teddy, is sitting next to me. Grandfather is tall. Dressed in black. With a white shirt and tie. He towers over everything in view.

Childhood Memories

The setting for this image is a four story brick row house at 15 West 127St. in Harlem. My grandfather and his children live here after the death of my grandmother Edith, who died soon after I was born. I am about eight or nine years old. My mother and my Aunt Edith are preparing me to visit Grandfather, whose sleeping quarters and study are on the second floor. This visit, as all Grandfather visits, is a special occasion requiring special clothes and especially good manners. I am entering his study and noticing shelves of books. Grandfather is wearing a black vest over his white shirt and tie. He has a mass of curly white hair. I don't recall any conversation. I do remember that he gives me money. When I think back about the number of his own children, plus my mother and brother living at 15 W 127th St. at that time, I understand why he had a sanctuary of his own.

Consider, if you will, that he had thirteen children, in all. My father, George, was the oldest. While a number of his children died in infancy, the Harlem household at the time of this visit was chaotic. Since, my grandmother, Edith, died soon after my birth; my mother became the caretaker for a houseful of children, until the first of a series of stepmothers (two of whom were sisters) came on board.

Girlhood

In this image, I am about 10 years old, living on a large estate in Connecticut with my parents, who worked for the German owners. My grandfather on this occasion is doing the visiting. His formal attire, bowler hat and all, is a sharp contrast to the wooded, stonewall country side.

Adolescent Memories

In this scene, I am a teenager living with my mother and brother in Montclair, New Jersey, where we eventually settled after leaving Connecticut. Recollections of Grandfather, at this time, are visits when he drives over from Harlem in his big black motor car bringing a number of my aunts and uncles to spend the day. There is Uncle Eddy, Uncle Josh, Uncle Reggie, Aunt Edith, Aunt Ruth, and Aunt Hope. He treats my mother, Gilla, as the responsible favorite daughter. In this scene, he is very much a family man even as he maintains a special authoritative reserve. Somehow, his very presence puts everyone on their best behavior yet they all appear to be having a good time together.

By now I am beginning to realize a softer side of him.

Young Adult Memories

In this image, I am about twenty one years old. Grandfather, is driving me home to New Jersey after I finished Harlem Hospital Nurses Training School. We are comfortable together in the ride across the Hudson, but not saying much. I feel appreciation for his help in getting packed and moved out of the nurse's residence.

Adulthood

I saw very little of him in my adult years. The last contact I had with him was when I took my infant daughter, Allyson, to Harlem to visit him in 1950. He was then an elderly gentleman living in a grand brownstone in upper Harlem. Warm and mellow as a toasted marshmallow, in bathrobe and slippers. We finally bonded.

I learned later in life that Grandfather was formally educated as a minister in Barbados by a missionary named Hartman. He traveled throughout the Caribbean and in South America before he was invited to New York City in 1911 to establish in New York City churches patterned after the Christian Mission of the West Indies.

The following is what I learned about him, mainly from my mother.

He had 13 children, (my father, George Hartman Farnum, was the first) and four wives (two were sisters). He was pastor of four churches in New York City, at one time. In addition to Bible study, he taught music, art and even sports. He was an artist, who painted a scroll 40 ft long, depicting biblical scenes, (which is on film in the Schomburg Library Collection, representing art work of Caribbean immigrants to New York City in the early 1900's.)

His life has been written about in other sources for those who want to know more.

Gloria Wheatley Johnson, born in the 1920s

"In a few weeks, Ebenezer would be having its first service in a beautiful new building."

Gloria Johnson retired from a career as a public school teacher and administrator. Her first recollection is of the church before it moved to the block where she grew up; and, she later recalls when the church would move from the residential brownstone to a large house of worship.

***

One of my earliest memories of Ebenezer (I was about 4 or 5 years old) was on a Sunday morning when I was walking with my mother and my Aunt Maude to 405 Lenox Avenue. I looked at every crevice on the sidewalk to see if I could find my pocketbook that I had lost the prior Sunday. Alas, I never found it! Of course, at that time, we referred to the church as The Christian Mission.

A much later memory was in my late teens, riding the bus home from Hunter College. I used to make sure that I sat on the right side of the vehicle, where I could see the building at 225 Lenox Avenue. In a few weeks, Ebenezer would be having its first service in a beautiful new building.

What goes around comes around! With God's blessing it certainly did happen that Ebenezer was able to secure the new building and keep it all these years.

Waldo Waterman, born in the 1930s

"Concerts at Ebenezer ... featured challenging classical works that required months of rehearsals."

Waldo Waterman still sings baritone with church choirs and choral groups around New York City.

***

I entered the United States in September, 1960, and my first church was Ebenezer Gospel Tabernacle at 225 Lenox Avenue. Although I was 30 years old, I attended Sunday school there every week, and was the student of Mrs. Malvina Gill, along with the Callender brothers, who were also adults at the time. At Ebenezer, Sunday school was not only for children; in fact, adults may even have been the majority in attendance. And just like the children, we had to learn our Bible memory verses each week.

Sunday school was after morning worship, and a large percentage of people remained all day for Sunday evening services, or returned after dinner at home. Evening services began with spirited congregational singing. Luther Allman, Jr. accompanied on the piano. A soloist or the church choir would usually sing at these services.

Afterwards, and interspersed sometimes with choruses, members stood one by one and gave testimonies about their Christian life. A few times each year, one of the auxiliaries would sponsor a major concert on Sunday evening, and service would be pre-empted. Rev. Luther Allman was director of the Tabernacle Chorus, in addition to being pastor of the church. I had been a church soloist back home in Barbados, and it wasn't long before I became one of the soloists with the Ebenezer Tabernacle Chorus.

I recently found the printed programs from the 12th annual concert sponsored by the Men's League of Ebenezer Gospel Tabernacle. I note the date was Sunday, June 25, 1967 – the same month and day that Ebenezer is now celebrating its 100th anniversary. June was always the month for the major concert at the church. The attendance for the performance that afternoon was 400 persons. All the seats in the sanctuary and the balcony were occupied, and chairs for the overflow crowd had to be put in the aisles, in the balcony. In the heat of June, without electric fans or air conditioning, and with every light bulb burning in the chandeliers and balcony light fixtures, the audience used their own fans, or the printed programs, or fans provided by nearby funeral homes.

Concerts at Ebenezer were sponsored by the Ladies Aid and the Men's League, and always featured challenging classical works, that required months of rehearsals, such as Handel's *Messiah, The Sermon on the Mount,* and *the Elijah,* by Felix Mendelssohn.

On that June, we performed the oratorio, *The Creation,* by Joseph Haydn. The female soloists were sopranos Inez Luke, Daphne Morgan, and Evelyn Simmonds; and male soloists were Oscar Newton, tenor, Waldo Waterman, baritone, and Rupert Bartlett, bass. Professor Felix Boyce and Hilda Murray accompanied the Tabernacle Chorus on pipe organ and piano, respectively.

People representing many churches made up the crowd. Some of the soloists were guest artists from other Harlem churches, and they had their own following, people eager to hear them tackle the challenging classical music sung at these concerts. Mr. Newton attracted members from Mount Olivet Baptist Church, where he was tenor soloist. Evelyn Simmonds was soloist at St. Ambrose Episcopal church, where I eventually also served as a soloist in their choir. After singing at St. Ambrose on Sunday mornings, I would walk over to Ebenezer for Sunday school classes, held in the afternoons. Daphne Morgan was a member of Grace Gospel Chapel. Hilda Murray belonged to the Church of the Illumination and Felix Boyce was organist in a church in Brooklyn.

It was church policy *not* to sell tickets for admission. Only freewill offerings were collected for events they held. After the concerts, refreshments were served in the downstairs fellowship hall. Favorites were codfish cakes and slices of carrot cake, prepared by Sis. Inez Luke and Sis. Eunice Waterman. Ginger beer and mauby were the beverages served.

I worked as a printer for most of my years in New York, and, my company moved to the World Trade Center in the 1980s. After surviving both bombings there, in 1993 and in 2001, I decided it was time to retire. By God's grace, I am alive to tell the story.

Rev. Carl O. Callender, Esq, born in the 1930s

"...Because of my experiences in the Ebenezer Sunday School, I learned to appreciate that Christianity is truly an everyday experience.... Ebenezer has played a principal role in helping make the world a better place"

Rev. Carl O. Callender was ordained to the gospel ministry at Ebenezer and served as General Superintendent of the Christian Mission in the 1980s. He still serves as an associate pastor in a Brooklyn church. He also retired as judge in the New York courts, and long-time provider of legal services for the poor. An advocate for housing for the poor and those of moderate income, he was assistant commissioner in New York City's agency responsible for preserving and developing housing.

Although holiness churches tended to look askance at the possibilities of a Christian being a lawyer, and maintaining his or her ethical standards, Carl Callender not only proved that Christian faith was motivation for serving others in their search for justice, but also inspired a generation of younger, Christian lawyers, who still serve in the New York City area.

He credits his upbringing at Ebenezer as critical to his many achievements.

***

Ebenezer is where I first found Christ at the age of six. I still remember going to the altar to accept Christ. I remember going to the Panama Christian Mission to be baptized. The issue at that time was whether children so young could be expected to understand what knowing Christ was all about.

From then on, my brother, Clive, and I attended prayer meeting and Bible study every week. I remember the times with Brother Leachman Greenidge and Brother Wall. I remember the dynamic messages of Rev. Charles Allman; the Sunday school lessons of Sister Malvina Gill; and, the deep insight provided by Pastors Farnum and Luther B. Allman Sr.

It was the devotion of my aunt Ella Waterman that kept me attentive to the word of God and the principles of the Ebenezer Church. All that I am today is because of what I learned at the Christian Mission. My sisters Pola and Gloria attended with me, and through them and the members of Ebenezer I discovered the wonders of God and the real meaning of the Gospel.

Because of my experiences in the Ebenezer Sunday School, I truly learned to appreciate that Christianity is an everyday experience. Bro. William Green taught Clive and me to appreciate true discipleship. He walked us home from the weekly Bible study and prayer meetings. He demonstrated what true love and fellowship is really all about. It was those early experiences at Ebenezer that gave me an understanding of the things that are truly valuable in life. I have carried those spiritual principles with me throughout all of my life.

Because of it, my life has been one of purpose as well as accomplishments. My brother Clive, who is now an outstanding kidney transplant surgeon, followed Christ with me and, because of what he learned from Ebenezer, has always been a phenomenal witness to me of what Christ in action is truly all about. Wherever he goes he never forgets to tell others about how the Christ he learned about at Ebenezer has transformed his life and made the impossible a reality in his life.

Inspiring moments

One of my most inspiring moments at Ebenezer happened when Clive and I were probably about eighteen. Clive had already had tuberculosis and had gone through a year at a hospital to recover from the then very dreaded disease. He went back to school, completed high school and college. He had applied to medical school. At that time we were sure the costs were too high for poor folks like us. Clive insisted that God would make a way. I persisted that God is good, but some things are too difficult and sometimes we have to be realistic. Some things were just not meant to be. We can't expect the impossible. Clive insisted that God would make a way somehow and see him through.

Clive was accepted into medical school. However, he did not even have bus fare to make it to school. I implored him to be reasonable and pursue other avenues. I explained that even now he did not have the fare to make it to school that Monday. He resisted, stating that God would see him through. On that Saturday, I tried to make him see that, at the point very close to Monday, he still did not have the money and we saw no way to get the money for his fare to school. I remember stating the same to him the Sunday before we were going to church at Ebenezer that morning. He repeated that God would make a way.

We went to church and Pastor Luther B. Allman took up an offering to help Clive as he journeyed to medical school. The amount of that offering was just enough to cover Clive's transportation costs to medical college. Clive went to medical college that Monday and graduated first in his class a few years later. All because of what he learned at Ebenezer. That God would see him through no matter how things seemed, and no matter how great the obstacles. That great faith in God was what we learned at Ebenezer

Who could ask for more as one embarked on the journey of life?

Were it not for Ebenezer, I would not be alive today. Most of the people that I grew up with have died long ago. I would be with them. But for the discipline I learned through the Christian love shown me by my brother and sisters who demonstrated the true example or model of Christ in their daily lives. My aunt Ella, my sisters Pola and Gloria grew up at Ebenezer. Our true roots were grounded through the love and ministry of the Ebenezer Christian Mission at 225 Lenox Avenue.

One of the plays that were written by Marilyn Allman Maye at Ebenezer is called: "What are you going to do about the world situation?" Well, Ebenezer has played a principal role in helping make the world a better place. It was through Ebenezer that so many outstanding individuals have made a substantial impact in this world. Ebenezer has done very much about this world situation. For those reasons, I am and shall be eternally grateful.

An unforgettable recollection

We were at an all-night prayer meeting. Clive and I were probably about ten years old. Present were Brothers Simeon Wall, Leachman Greenidge, and William Green. Sister Isaac, and Bro. Felix Allman were also present. Of course Pastor Luther B. Allman was also present. I will never forget the people marching around, especially the men singing:

The fight is on, Oh Christian soldiers.
And face to face in stern array.
With colors streaming the right and wrong engage today.
The fight is on so be not weary.
Be strong and in his might hold fast.
If God is for us, His banner over us,
We'll sing the victor's song at last.

Seeing those brothers marching around the church and singing that song has been my continuing inspiration when ever times were tough and things seemed impossible. This event took place at least 65 years ago. Yet it has left an indelible impression upon me.

I will eternally thank God for the difference Ebenezer has made in my life.

Clive O. Callender, M.D., born in the 1930s

"I recall ... hearing ... preaching about the virtues of addressing the souls of mankind and their bodies as well. It was then that I decided I would become a medical missionary."

Dr. Callender is a world-renown kidney transplant surgeon and university professor, who never fails to credit his years at Ebenezer as the underpinnings of his numerous accomplishments. He has travelled the globe, and appeared throughout the media, advocating for equal access to kidney transplantation for the poor. He still leads a non-profit organization dedicated to awareness and support for minority organ transplantation. He has trained a generation of surgeons, and saved countless lives through surgery, in the United States, the Caribbean, and West Africa.

His recollections of his childhood at Ebenezer begin with humor, and proceed to the more serious.

***

I recall at the age of seven, along with my twin brother Carl, crawling and playing under and between the seats in the middle of the church service. I recall at the same age hearing Reverend Eustace Farnum and Reverend Luther Benjamin Allman Sr., preaching about the virtues of addressing the souls of mankind and their bodies as well. It was then that I decided I would become a medical missionary.

A scientist and a musician, Dr. Callender has always maintained a love for singing tenor, that was nurtured during years of singing in Ebenezer's choirs and vocal groups. He and his brother have recorded a CD with songs they love, in memory of their late aunt, Mrs. Ella Waterman:

> I recall singing in the choir under Rev. Allman's leadership and performing the Hallelujah Chorus. This was one of the highlights of my life as a tenor in the Ebenezer choir.
>
> I remember most vividly singing and rehearsing and singing many solos with the tutelage and organ and piano artistry of child prodigy, Luther Benjamin Allman Jr., when I was between the age of 12 and 20. I remember the music and soprano solos of Lorna Granderson and Sister Inez Luke, and the singing of the Seale Sisters.

Finally, he reflects on the influences of those lay persons whose lives and teaching made an indelible impression.

> I recall the testimonies of Sister Isaac; ... the tutelage of Sister Malvina Gill, my Sunday school teacher; and, Brother William Green, who was like a father to me.

Luther Allman, born in the 1940s

"... the Church ... was more central to the daily life of our families, than even our homes or jobs"

A gifted musician since childhood, Luther Allman has served as organist in churches in New York, Seattle, and Los Angeles, and still consults nationally for the organ industry. Now retired from a career in business, he is a prolific producer of gospel and jazz keyboard music.

***

I have only a vague memory of the church when it was located at 15 West 127th Street ... then I remember when they bought the former synagogue at 121st and Lenox and my father going over every day to scrape off the Hebrew lettering that was all around the Nave, and parts of the ceiling and walls. I think you can still see some of the old lettering on the walls in some places. The purchase of the synagogue signaled the last vestiges of white home ownership in the surrounding area. Since observant Jews had to live close enough to walk to their house of worship, obviously the congregants lived close by in the surrounding neighborhood. The synagogue was available to be sold to Ebenezer, only because their congregants had fled Harlem to escape the swelling migration of blacks from the midtown west-side area, northward to Harlem.

About that same time we moved from our apartment on 131st street to our home at 11 East 124th St., I must have been about 3 or 4 yrs. old, so that would be about 1944. During that time I remember my maternal Uncle David coming home in his World War 2 uniform and the fuss they made over his safe return. I remember the yearly church body gatherings in Manhattan and Brooklyn on alternate Labor Days. We had no car in those days nor TVs, so the radio was our primary entertainment outside of church, and the subway was our primary form of transportation.

To say church was entertaining is an understatement! The characters that we called Brother and Sister so-and-so, would make any modern day sit-com or reality show, green with envy! What I remember vividly was the clash of the two cultures that we were a part of – the West Indian culture was the culture of our church family, and the American culture was that of the dominant society. We had to learn to wend our way and negotiate very carefully and skillfully between the two.

Almost every day of the week was some form of church-related activity – from the Monday night home prayer meetings, Bible studies, Friday night choir rehearsals, to multiple services on Sunday with afternoon Open-Air services on the corner in the summer. The church was truly our safe-haven!

Looking back, the Church environment was more central to the daily life of our families, than even our homes or jobs. It seemed normal at the time, and I believe this is how it must have been with the early Biblical church – where the disciples "had everything in common" and met daily for prayer, worship, consolation, protection and fasting. I would not be surprised if that all-encompassing environment at Ebenezer was modeled after the practices of the early church congregations.

Besides the sound Bible-based teachings, the musical activities were unusually plentiful and ongoing. The music department was noted for the choral extravaganzas each holiday season. Before I was born, there was also a full orchestra that performed for the services as well as on the outside occasionally. I think World War 2 was the time when the church orchestra ceased to function as it regularly had. But the choir tradition continued on, and my earliest memories included those weekly rehearsals and choral singing at holiday seasons. This is the musical heritage I received at Ebenezer that has stood with me and stayed with me, and will be with me all the years of my life – for this I am eternally grateful.

My father was a self-taught cornetist, a musical conductor, a solfeggio singer, a connoisseur of sacred choral and operatic works, a voracious reader, a master of daily completing the difficult NY Times crossword puzzle, an amateur electrician, plumber, and painter – all of these self-taught gifts were shared with and gifted to Ebenezer during the 72 years he was a member and the 50 years our mother was a member.

Our parents being married in the church, and their love for the church and all it represented, as well as the love of all the other member families, is the reason why we can celebrate this 100th anniversary in their stead. They are looking down, hopefully pleased at what has transpired since they departed and what may lay ahead for this church.

Strong male role models

I remember when the church mortgage was burned and how many of the membership wept openly from joy and gratitude to God that this huge financial obligation involving much personal sacrifice, was finally over. I'll always remember in particular, Brother/Deacon Arnold Jones weeping uncontrollably at the burning ceremony. What an impression that must have made on me that I still remember it all these 60+ years that have gone by, like it was just yesterday.

Another notable aspect of Ebenezer was the plethora of strong male role-models who were dignified, competent and solid as a rock. This is contrasted with the typical church today where the females outnumber the males by several multiples.

I'll always remember favorites of mine like Brothers Grant, Fagan, Wall, Jones, Shepherd, Gibbs, Whitehead, Kirton, the Allman uncles, numerous relatives, Brothers Bartlett, Greenidge, and others. My musical influences include Felix Boyce, Mrs. Newton, Mr. Newton, Bro. Bartlett, and of course, the female backbones of the church, without which there would be no church as we knew it.

Grace Allman Burke, R.N., ThD, born in the 1940s

" [some] sayings ... made us young people collapse with hysterical laughter and almost fall under the benches, despite the disapproving and staring eyes of our parents..."

Dr. Grace Allman Burke is retired from a four-decades-long career in women's health, during which she served as a certified nurse midwife, a nursing professor, and an international health consultant in the Caribbean and South America. Ordained as a minister of the gospel, she is an author and conference speaker.

***

During the 1940s, the decade of my birth, and in the decade thereafter, Harlem was a simple, yet complex place in which to grow up. People were very much a church-going bunch, you knew your neighbors well and Mt. Morris Park was a safe place in which to play. The scourge of drugs had not yet infiltrated our lives, but alcohol and gambling played a significant role within some neighborhood families. We, the children of West Indian immigrants, were strongly encouraged to pursue an education as we grew up. Not going to college was not an option. However, our teachers at school, predominantly Caucasian, relentlessly tried to discourage us, citing a quick general or commercial diploma from high school as our ultimate goal.

At home we were served Caribbean meals daily, yet we loved the taste of cornbread and collard greens from our friends and colleagues of Southern origin. We were dazzled by, to us, the bright lights of 125th

Street. The Apollo Theatre called to us as we wended our way to school and church. Fats Domino, Nat King Cole, Ray Charles and Ella Fitzgerald dominated the airwaves with their soulful tunes. The church insisted, however, that gospel and classical music and the old hymns of the church were the ones to get us through. Negro people, as we were called at that time, could shop at Blumstein's and other stores in the area, but were not allowed to serve as cashiers there.

We were taught in school to be fiercely loyal to our country and to the flag. Yet the Korean War raged abroad, conscripting several of my cousins in combat, with a cause that we didn't understand. Here at home, we heard a desperate call for freedom by our black brothers and sisters in the South, who were still locked in the chains of segregation.

Martin Luther King visited us in Harlem, asking us to join them in the fight. Elijah Muhammed and Malcolm X brought the Black Muslims to Harlem with their calls of "Muhammed Speaks!" Daddy Grace and Father Divine told us that they were God incarnate and that worshipping them would get us through the pearly gates.

It was against this cultural, social and political backdrop that my days at Ebenezer began. I was one of the first infants dedicated to the Lord at the church's present location at 121st Street and Lenox Avenue. Looking back, I can see that the principles and precepts taught me at Ebenezer Christian Mission during the first three decades of my life, made an indelible and life-long impression that pursue me to this day.

***

My earliest recollections of Ebenezer date back to the late 1940s. I remember being a little girl in Sis. Ruth Francis' Sunday school class. An elderly lady with long, lily-white hair drawn back into a bun, she was very light complexioned, her hands displaying aging arteries and veins. Her fingers were gnarled, no doubt twisted from arthritis. She was an immigrant from the South American country of Suriname, which is next to Guyana. Sis. Francis loved children and taught the little girls' class. My classmates were Janet and Carol Seale, Millicent Neal, Peggy-Ann Facey-Smith, among others. We all loved Sis. Francis. She was sweet and kind and was very interested in us coming to know Jesus. We all joined in as, in unison with the other Sunday school classes, we sang our standard opening hymn,

"We're marching to Zion, beautiful, beautiful Zion, we're marching upward to Zion, the beautiful City of God!"

After settling in with the usual greetings to each other, Sis. Francis distributed our Sunday school cards—very colorful ones—with our lesson for the day. We listened with rapt attention as she taught us, through the story, the wonderful Word of God. Occasionally, we girls would glance over at the boys' class, taught by Sis. Malvina Gill. We'd giggle as they sat there staring into space, seemingly bored and anxious for it all to be over. By the time the Sunday School Superintendent called the classes to attention, we girls were ready to recite and reflect on what we had learned. Sis. Francis' girls almost always got it right!

Another vivid memory was my fascination with the older women of the church during the early 1950s. My dad, Rev. Luther Allman, was the pastor by then and my mom, Sis. Daisy Allman was the church mother. The ladies had vivid personalities, with ideas of their own which they were determined to project on us younger girls. I loved to watch how they dressed and was always listening to snatches of their conversations.

Crowns

All of the ladies wore hats—everywhere to every occasion. It needn't be just to Sunday morning service; even at picnics their hats could be seen. In their minds, a lady wasn't properly dressed unless she had on a hat. Gloves were also an integral part of the couture. But a hat was a requirement to enter the church. "A woman with her head uncovered" was in direct disobedience to God's laws. Sleeveless dresses in those days, were totally out of the question. Women in pants were an abomination. Those who wore them were going straight to hell. Jewelry was a sign of a Jezebel spirit and lipstick signaled your desire to "look like the world." It didn't matter how we girls left home under our mothers' watchful eye-- when we arrived at the church, some church lady would be there to inspect us on arrival and was sure to comment about what we were wearing. My mom wasn't always pleased with their assessment but those were the times.

One of my favorite pastimes was to sneak downstairs to the church kitchen where the Ladies Aid was preparing the meal for the church members after service. I'd pretend to be going to the restroom and stand, sight unseen, in a corner without uttering a word. After all, children should be seen and not heard! I'd listen as they joked about the folks upstairs—who could sing well and who couldn't; whose hat was on sideways; whose slip was hanging during the altar call; who couldn't preach worth a dime and why he was even asked to do so on that particular Sunday, was beyond them. They laughed uproariously when once the visiting preacher's teeth fell out onto his Bible. Sometimes the gossip got real juicy and I'd bend my ear to get all of the details. I remember vividly that on one occasion one of the ladies caught me listening. "A kid is in our midst!" she called out as I sprinted quickly back upstairs.

The crowning glory for the Ladies Aid was the spread they prepared for the annual Labor Day Fellowship service. They'd first participate in the song service upstairs, dancing in the aisles with hands upraised, shouting "When we all get to heaven what a day of rejoicing that will be!" Then they'd go downstairs, donning their aprons, putting the finishing touches on the feast.

During the late 1950s the church members raised the bar higher for us young people. We were required to attend Young People's meetings. Elvina Coulthurst, escorted my brother, sister and me to those Sunday evening services. Our elders were determined that we would be armed with the sword of the Spirit, which is the Word of God. We were drilled with scripture facts during Vacation Bible School. We "advanced arms,"[48] reciting nuggets from sacred text. The Callender twins, Carl and Clive, my brother, Luther Jr. and I were all members of the citywide inter-church Bible contest. We were fierce opponents as we competed against neighboring churches like Ephesus Seventh Day Adventist. We beamed with pride as we listened to ourselves winning the contests which were pre-recorded over the radio. Having a black and white television was a luxury in those days.

***

My most favorite memory, however, was of Tuesday night Testimony Meetings at Ebenezer. Here, we were enjoined to stand and relate what the Lord had done for us over the past week. This was when we learned some of the most intimate details of the lives of our parishioners. They left nothing unsaid. Sometimes they sung a verse, many times off-key, from a gospel chorus of the day, and then sat down. Others sang *and* gave their testimony. One of my classic recollections was the lady who encountered a thief as she made her way to church. In a strongly lilting Caribbean accent she advised us:

"Beloved, I just had to stand and give praise to God tonight. As I waited by the bus-stop, a robber tried to grab my pocket book. But I called out to Jesus and held on! He ran off with the pocket but I kept the book!"

It was sayings like these that made us young people collapse with hysterical laughter and almost fall under the benches despite the disapproving and staring eyes of our parents. I could go on and on but I'll stop here, with these glorious memories of my coming of age at Ebenezer.

Rev. Gloria W. Nurse, born in the 1940s

"...it was because of their fervent prayers on my behalf that I survived another brutal asthma attack."

Rev. Gloria Nurse is an ordained minister and associate pastor in a church in Washington, D.C. She shares how central her experiences at Ebenezer are to her vision of ministry.

***

As a little girl attending Ebenezer Gospel Tabernacle, located at the corner of 121st Street and Lenox Avenue, was exciting. I loved attending church on Sundays, and how well I remember the special aura that was Sunday mornings at Ebenezer. As the individuals entered the sanctuary, they were not only dressed for church, but each one brought with them a bold witness of the awesomeness of what Psalms 139 calls being "fearfully and wonderfully made."

At that time, however, I had other words to describe some of the people who attended Ebenezer...

To explain each of the personalities of the people who attended Ebenezer Gospel Tabernacle, one would need Webster's Dictionary and Roget's Thesaurus, because the entire volumes of encyclopedias could not contain the colorful array of their uniqueness. The various West Indian island people who came to the United States brought with them not only their culture and moral values, but also many other customs. Their one-of-a-kind dress styles, lyrical language lingo, musical capabilities, and intellectual prowess combined with an unwavering commitment to God. Yet, their defiant refusal to embrace some of the American traditions and customs as their own was met with a fierce, holy resistance that the Taliban would have admired and employed among their own warfare tactics.

***

The Bible says that "laughter is medicine for the heart" and in Ebenezer Gospel Tabernacle some took the meaning of this scripture to another level. One such person in our church was a sister who routinely finished quoting the scriptures for the Pastor before he could finish reading the text. She was ready to help him preach his sermon, whatever the text, and even before he could utter the first sentence from his lips. Sister Keturah Isaac hailed from the Virgin Islands and was a small 4 ft 8 in, frail-looking woman, with a singsong accent and a distinctive voice that could be heard by all. She started every testimony with a song. Not trained musically, she sang in a way that allowed no one to join in, because her rhythms were unpredictable, and her lyrics improvised. One of her favorite songs started off with: *"I've got a mansion right over the hilltop, where the streets are paved with gold."* The rest of the song was pure vintage Sister Isaac; she would then improvise the rest of the 4 verses of the song with her own lyrics and rap. Her song continued with phrases like.. *" I got me peas and me rice and me jam and me butter and I'm going home to that land where I'll never grow old---Oooo I gotta mansion right over the hilltop."* The next words she uttered after singing four verses in their entirety, was "Beloved" or "Saints", as she turned to address the congregation.

All of us at church knew then that no comedy writer or comedian could compare or equal the natural ability, style, words that would effortlessly flow out of Sister Isaac's mouth during her one-woman testimony time. We knew rap before Jay Zee got paid for it.

Those of us who were forced to attend Sunday Night services knew that the Ed Sullivan show which started at the same 8p.m. hour each week, could never rival the natural talent of the people in our church

One day she truly shocked us. It was our annual Thanksgiving Service which was held early on that particular Thursday and she was late arriving to the church. As she got up to give her Thanksgiving testimony that day, she began in a most unusual way. She shocked each one of us that day by telling us she just "shot someone today." We sat there in stunned silence as she began to tell us that she had to go into her holster, retrieve her gun and shoot a man through the heart. She claimed she shot him "through and through." She continued to shoot him, " in the heart until he dropped dead." We knew Sister Isaac was capable, strong and an intense, fearless woman, who no one in their right mind would mess with. We also knew that many of these strong women could truly put anyone down with just a look. Absolutely no one, thought of messing with these unique and inspired women of God.

We younger people wouldn't underestimate those church sisters. We knew the story of another church woman who used to take the short cuts through the park at night to get home after leaving her church. One night, in the middle of an attack by a would-be robber, instead of being afraid, she began to sing to him in a loud voice "The Lord is my light and my salvation of WHOM shall I be afraid?" She then told the man to kneel down and accept the Lord. The poor man was so shocked and afraid that he turned around and ran out of the Mt. Morris Park (currently known as Marcus Garvey Park), completely forgetting his task, the robbery. Legend has it that he is still running around the park. Now, back to Sister Isaac's Thanksgiving testimony.

Worried that there might be a corpse, somewhere, the victim of Sister Isaac's gun violence, we were soon made to understand that her purse was the holster, the Bible was her shotgun, and that, she had shot the word of God through her unsuspecting villain, as the word "pierces the heart." The church erupted in laughter. The pianist collapsed at the keyboard, and others could be seen falling to the floor in hysterical laughter. She did not crack a smile, as she continued with her testimony. She told us that she told the man that "he could be resurrected from the dead through the acceptance of the Lord Jesus Christ entering into his wounded and sinful heart." I don't know if this man wanted to come back to life through the resurrection power of Jesus Christ, but I do know that there will never be another Sister Isaac who will tread this universe again…after all she's in her mansion, just over the hilltop, where the streets are paved in gold and she'll never grow old.

***

In every church, there are always a few people who will stay deeply engraved in your spirit and memory. Such is the case with Ebenezer Gospel Tabernacle. Some of these people have challenged us to be serious about our commitment to Christ. Others have fed our minds and hearts with stories from the Bible that we will long remember. There are those who have inspired us to raise our standards and expectations of ourselves to achieve what we never thought we could. There are so many wonderful stories about church members, whom God has used in our lives in unexpected ways.

The person who represented quite an authoritarian figure, without being a dictator, and whom I viewed as having the highest intellectual acumen was my Pastor, Luther Benjamin Allman. His regal, upright bearing and the sound of his voice preaching every Sunday reached my small ears and affected my spirit in an unseen way at the time. Rev. Allman represented many things to me. He was not only my pastor, but he was a father figure without realizing it. His love for music, cultural sophistication, spiritual giftedness and his vast political knowledge instilled within me a love for those things also. Like many of the West Indians of his generation his quest for knowledge had no limitations. I was soon to find out how far his intellectual curiosity would extend.

One night as his daughter, Marilyn, and I sat at their dinner table, he wanted to look at the evening news. He turned on the TV, while the news anchor's voice informed us of current events around the nation. Everyone looked at a blackened TV screen as if they were truly watching the news. What made this extremely memorable to me was the fact that no one at the table flinched or acted as if anything was amiss when only the sound came on and not the picture. As I sat at that table I was having a bit of trouble with this picture in my own mind. Is this family normal? Am I truly crazy? Am I missing something? Why is the entire family watching this picture-less TV as though it was the most normal thing? Marilyn, noticing my confusion, politely informed me that the television had been broken for a while and that her father dutifully turned it on every evening to listen to it, looking at the blank screen as though this was the custom for everyone. While trying to stifle her laughter, we both excused ourselves from the dining table and headed upstairs to her bedroom. She explained to me that this unusual aspect of watching TV represented "normal behavior," in a household more interested in the content of the news, than in its packaging.

A vision of ministry

Every summer we had bus excursions to various state parks throughout the tri-state area. These summer outings were filled with fun, laughter, eating at each other's tables, games and swimming. I went swimming that particular Saturday and, although not feeling well due to my asthma, I had a great time and did not inform anyone that I was feeling ill. At the end of the picnic, I could tell that I was getting worse but thought that I could make it back home. As the buses journeyed back to New York City from the distant Long Island seashores, I knew I was in deep trouble. I passed out and the bus stopped as I was rushed to the hospital in Huntington, Long Island. They treated me in the emergency room and released me. Pastor Allman was there with me in the emergency room and drove me back in his car to the bus because I wanted to be with all my friends. To my surprise, not only had they waited for me, but also, it was because of their fervent prayers on my behalf that I survived another brutal asthma attack. Pastor Allman allowed me to get back on that bus but made sure to drive me home upon our arrival back at the church. He cared for me and showed his watchful concern for me on every level. Today, Pastoral Care is a required course in seminary.

Pastor Allman whose pastoral call came from the Lord had more training than many who have gone through seminary because he cared for his flock with tender care, compassion and love. His concern was for his congregation and how he could serve them, rather than for himself. He was not a man to worry about how the congregation would care for him and what they could do for him. His mission in life emanated from his Christ-centered focus on, "doing for others." Because of his compassion, care and intellectual capabilities, combined with so many other gifts, Pastor Allman to me represented the gift that keeps on giving. I am so very proud to have been given the honor to call him PASTOR, because he truly represented the call of a true Pastor in every dimension and facet of his life.

Marilyn C. Maye, Ed.D., born in the 1940s

"They arranged their lives to live nearby; when they purchased homes, they made sure it was in the church's neighborhood, because they were there almost every evening of the week"

Marilyn Maye is a lifelong educator, serving as classroom teacher, school district administrator, and university professor in New York and New Jersey. An author and educational consultant, she still serves in church lay leadership and on boards of non-profit organizations.

***

It was the early 1950s, former General Dwight Eisenhower was elected President after achieving fame in World War II. It cost 10 cents to ride a bus or subway (the price had gone up from a nickel to a dime, in 1948, the year I was born) in New York City. Working-class whites were moving to the suburbs as they experienced huge economic gains, because of government programs for veterans such as the GI Bill, which provided the money for new homes and paid college tuition. Those that stayed in the outer boroughs got their children educated for free; tuition was $0 for all students at New York City's public colleges, although acceptance patterns ensured that mostly whites went during the day, and blacks went at night.

Public schools in New York were virtually segregated, not by law, but by policy and by segregated living patterns. Growing up in Harlem, I knew which stores on 125th Street were off-limits to blacks; it was 1957 before history was made and a major corporation hired a black executive, Jackie Robinson, recently retired from professional baseball, and blacks felt as though they had a stake in a major business, the popular luncheonette chain, Chock Full o' Nuts, on 7th Avenue. If stores didn't outright refuse to serve black customers, you could expect to be treated rudely and to be followed around as you shopped, even by some black employees who felt lucky enough to work like glorified servants for their white bosses.

But, who, at the time, understood why these issues were important? As I skipped and jumped along the sidewalks on my way to elementary school at P. S. 68 on West 127th Street, I was the happiest kid in the world. Maybe those people in the stores around the corner were rude to me, but, I was the darling of my family and my real community – the church family at Ebenezer Gospel Tabernacle on Lenox Avenue. It would be some years before we had a family auto. We walked the 6 blocks to church almost every evening of the week. Our maternal grandparents had a home on the west side of Mount Morris Park, and we passed it on our way to church. We walked to school. We walked to the markets to shop and walked home, three or four of us in the family each carrying two shopping bagsful. Sometimes the total grocery bill for all of that shopping was a whopping $19. That's not decimal error. Nineteen dollars could buy a week's worth of groceries. At thanksgiving and Christmastime, the bill might even go as high as $40!

***

We went to church and school with people just like us, and, if some of the older ones knew we were poor, they never told us younger ones. Our parents were working hard to let us know that we were just as good as anyone else, and that we needed to do our best in school and graduate and make something of ourselves. We knew that whatever careers we would pursue, the goal would be service. Our future work would involve helping other people; the idea of getting rich for its own sake, or to acquire material things was just as alien as the culture that our parents brought with them when they had immigrated to New York from places like Barbados, Panama, Cuba, Jamaica, Trinidad, and a variety of Caribbean islands. The English patois that they spoke sounded hysterically funny to us first-generation kids, born in the USA. We practiced speaking to each other in our version of their accented English, and it remains a staple of our conversation whenever we reflect on our childhoods.

The people at Ebenezer were our family. Most of the members of the Board, the Sunday school teachers, and auxiliary leaders lived within walking distance of the church. They arranged their lives to live nearby; when they purchased homes, they made sure it was in the church neighborhood, because they were there almost every evening of the week. The Greenidges lived on West 121st, the same block as the church; Bro. and Sis. Fagan lived on West 122nd, the Callenders lived at 271 Lenox Avenue, the Wheatleys and Whiteheads at 24 West 127th, the Allmans at 11 East 124th St., and so on. Some lived as far as Amsterdam Avenue, and could take the 101 bus down to 125th Street and Lenox and walk over to the church. In the wake of white flight from the cities, a few of the families had started to buy homes in the Bronx and in Corona in the outer boroughs, where blacks were just getting an opportunity to live in previously all-white neighborhoods like the Grand Concourse or Astoria Boulevard! Even before my father became pastor, in 1952, his siblings encouraged him to move to these outer boroughs, but, he had refused, because even as a lay member, he felt that he and his family should live as close to their church as possible. What if there were a blizzard and you couldn't get to the church! It was unthinkable.

One of the iconic memories of my childhood is accompanying Sis. Constance Bynoe, who had lost her vision late in life, as she went from her apartment on 128th Street and Madison Avenue, to church every Sunday morning. I inherited the unpaid job from my older siblings, who had felt equally mortified being seen by their schoolmates walking through our neighborhood with the elderly, blind lady on our arm. Of course, being blind had absolutely no effect on her determination to be at church every Sunday morning. I would arrive at the house, go upstairs and find her putting her last minute breakfast dishes away. She knew every inch of her apartment by heart, and could cook, eat and clean up her kitchen by feeling her way around. She carried a cane to church; but, she moved as though she knew every step along the 10 blocks or so. You didn't hold her arm; she held yours. And, after a long day at church, you walked her back home as well. In those days, there were limited services for people with disabilities; there was no federal law guaranteeing them accommodations. Neighbors, friends and church family were the social safety net; and, because everyone bought in, it worked, for the most part.

"...We knew that whatever careers we would pursue, the goal would be service."

We were also the recipients of a strong sense of communal obligation. That was the ethic among upwardly mobile black people in that era. Twin sisters, Gloria and Lenora Wheatley, were role models in our church family. They may have been the first in their families to achieve college degrees, and among the first in the church family. As youngsters watching them, we were exposed to the idea of a college education. Gloria had the distinction of having attended Hunter College as a day student, one of the most prestigious of the public colleges, and one that few blacks attended during the day. She became an elementary-grade teacher in the neighborhood school one block from her parents' home; and the school that several of us from the church attended. So, we had one of our own teaching in the school. We were so proud to know her. Very few teachers, or professionals of any kind, were black, and the school administration was almost entirely white and male. She could be counted on to monitor our academic progress for our parents and to provide tutoring, if necessary, to prepare us to take the tests for special schools, for Junior and Senior High School. She was a role model for what could be achieved, with her impeccable mastery of the English language, and her world travels. She lived in Harlem most of her adult life, as did most of the black middle class. Whether because of rampant segregation, or in spite of it, these first-in-their-families professionals were committed to service, and the young people in the community were exposed to what education could bring to one's life.

Our mother had gone back to work, after our father became full-time pastor. She was one of the few her age to have a professional degree – she had earned the registered nurse degree in 1937 from the all-black Lincoln School for Nurses at Lincoln Hospital in the Bronx, and had stopped working after a few years to raise her children. Our father had one of the best jobs a black man could have in those days – an employee of the federal government in the United States Postal Service. I found out years later, in college, that several of the fathers of my peers had also worked there. It was a top job for blacks, although they rarely had the positions that entailed them meeting customers at the sales windows or delivering mail on public streets. They worked in the back, in the invisible positions; but, they had opportunities to discuss world events, civil rights developments, and to meet other blacks and people of other ethnic groups. Although most of them did not have the opportunity to go to college, they had a work environment that broadened them; they had access to lots of important written material; and they had decent pay that enabled them to buy homes and send their children to schools in better neighborhoods.

After achieving the coveted status of government employee, when my father accepted the call to pastor the church at Ebenezer, he was taking a reduction in social status and a huge pay cut. He would be the first Ebenezer pastor to have an agreed-upon weekly salary, that wasn't whatever the offering taken in on Sunday could provide. He would be guaranteed $25 per week – that was a huge leap of faith for the church – that they could guarantee so much. The founding pastor, Elder Eustace Farnum, although he had had 8 or 9 children to raise, understood how difficult it could be for the family not to be able to depend on a minimum salary. He had worked for 40 years with whatever the church could give him. In addition to whatever the offering could provide, church members were expected to give supplementary gifts of food and clothing to the pastor's family. But, this kind of uncertainty left many clergy families with a lot of anxiety. My father's $25 weekly salary would remain in place for more than 15 years; it was a major commitment for the church to raise it to $50 per week in the late 1960s. Thankfully, my mother's salary made up the difference; I don't think Pastor Farnum's first wife had that option. When she died, he remarried twice, to women with no children and their own financial means.

***

Perhaps the aspect of our upbringing that I am most thankful for is the solid spiritual training that we received. There was never a doubt in my mind that our elders in the church were totally committed to their faith in Jesus Christ. A cynic might say, "what else could they do?" Church was truly the best part of their lives, otherwise spent as invisible people doing the menial jobs that made white America prosperous. Many of our leading women were domestics, whose white bosses would occasionally show up at church to hear them sing at a concert. The men were laborers, and expanded their income by real estate holdings. But, they were able to thrive, in a period when many of their urban neighbors were consumed by alcoholism, diseases, and poverty, exactly because of their disciplined pursuit of God's will for their lives. They invested their money in "the Lord's house," and confessed their faults when they slipped and fell.

They testified of their faith every Tuesday evening. Listening to these weekly testimonies, we kids could pretty much recite the favorite scriptures of each adult, and anticipate exactly how they would start or end their stories. Some, like founding member Bro. William Green, would always begin their testimonies with a chorus, *"I have a song that Jesus gave me, it was sent from Heaven above....In my heart their rings a melody of love."* They prayed together in home cottage meetings on Mondays and studied the scriptures at Bible Studies on Thursday evenings. Holidays provided special occasions for everyone to testify.

Although the tithes and offerings often came from meager earnings, Ebenezer members always supported missionaries who toiled in several countries in Africa, India, Cuba, and other parts of the world. Ebenezer was a must-stop church for missionaries home on furlough, seeking to raise funds to go back.

And, they were not disappointed. Ebenezer was always a place where you could get a good meal, and find people who cared about you and would pray for you, not just on Sunday, but throughout the week. That legacy is written in our DNA, and, thankfully, persists into the 21st century.

Who needs TV or the movies?

Becoming the pastor's children, we had a ringside seat to the comedies and tragedies of life among this mostly immigrant community, newly urban and trying to assimilate their families in the capital of Black America. Sooner or later, everyone came through our home. There was no pastor's office at the church; and, even in our home, our father only had a desk where he could keep his papers and some of his books. A room for counseling? What's that? So, people came through with their emergencies and crises, and called at all hours of the day and night. When you woke up in the morning, and walked to go to the bathroom, it was not unusual to have to pass a member of the church committee who had dropped by earlier than my wakeup time, to see my father about some pressing issue, or to bring some paperwork before going to the bank. "Good morning, Bro. Gibbs," as you wiped the "sleep" out of your eyes. Privacy? What was that? And, if someone came by with a hard-luck story about being thrown out of their room, or needing to go South to take care of a dying parent, we could be thrown out of our beds to accommodate the travelling guest.

We learned to keep our mouths shut; no matter how dire the emergency or family crisis, we could get wind of it, because no one really had privacy. But, we knew better than to breathe a word to anyone about anything we had overheard. So, we learned to keep confidences, as we realized the intensity of the dramas that faced the people in our church family. In retrospect, many of the stories seem humorous, but at the time, real crises were constant. Among them is the time, my father had to go to bail out an elderly church member who had shot a persistently annoying supervisor at work. Or, the time, an irate husband brought a gun to church and tried to shoot his wife in the kitchen! Then there were the undocumented immigrants who married solely to attain legal status; the weddings between older women and younger men, and how many grooms were there, at whose weddings someone would cry out when the pastor said, "If anyone knows a reason why this couple should not be wed, speak now or forever hold your peace." How many of them had legal or common-law wives in the islands, and children of all ages, that their prospective spouses knew nothing about? Oprah and Judge Judy have nothing on the dramas we saw!

In our own house, to help pay the mortgage (the house was bought for $18,000 in 1948, so the mortgage payments might have been $75 per month) my parents took in roomers – often single men who needed a place to live in the City so they could conveniently get to their jobs. Someone could write a novel based on the characters who lived in our brownstone, single-room occupancy, rooming house. It was not unusual for us to have as many as 25 people living there at a time. Some whole families lived in one large room, sharing a common bathroom with strangers. Several immigrant families spent their earlier years there; and, some African-American families who had migrated from places like Mississippi, also lived with us. I say "with us" because, although every room had a door that locked, because of the need to share washrooms, and the main entrance to the house, everyone knew what was going on with everyone else. Those who were not believers had to abide by the rules of the Christian owner. One night, my father busted one roomer that had his girlfriend sleeping over, telling him to find somewhere else to live his sinful lifestyle. Another one, whose girlfriend stayed too long too many evenings, eventually decided to marry her – and we all happily attended the wedding. We were in between family members who didn't get along with their kin; we were the protection agency for one elderly tenant whose greedy relatives tried to poison her to get their inheritance; we even had a racist, Swedish tenant who hated black people, and regularly referred to us as the N-word! What rich stories for a true life drama! And what solid preparation for careers in health care, education and business that we would eventually pursue, as well as for ministries we would engage, in the churches we would attend.

But, despite the low-life dramas around us, we were regulars at concerts of high culture and participants in choirs and orchestras, in Harlem and around New York City. We all took piano lessons, and, over the years, I've met several musicians who played in a community orchestra that my father conducted. I don't remember the name of the orchestra, and I'm still looking through local archives to find articles that I was told were written about their performances.

Although most of its early members had never attended a college, and many not even a high school, Ebenezer was a place of culture in the community and cooperated with other churches in putting on Handel's *Messiah* almost every year, with some of the best vocal artists in the black community. As in the original Jewish ghettos of 19th century Europe, the forced isolation of cultural groups produces tremendous opportunities for cross-pollination of great minds and talent. Momentous and global contributions were made by Jews like Marx, Freud and Einstein, who emerged after the ghettos were opened, so says Michael Goldfarb in his book, titled *Emancipation*. I am sure that history will show similar outcomes from the Harlem of the 20th century. Not enough books have yet been written about the wealth of talent in our community at that time.

I have attended some of the finest schools in America, and have not met many people I thought were better educated than my father. Although I'm an advocate for making schools as good as they can be, I'm grateful to have seen firsthand that someone can teach himself to master English grammar, classical literature and music, theology, the scriptures, and world history, and remain an intellectually curious, critical thinker until his dying day. At his funeral, he was eulogized as "a man who lived in the public library and spoke as though he'd eaten the dictionary!"

Roxanne Johnson Kent, born in the 1950s

"... the love and sense of family... have been a lifelong strength...."

In her career in public relations, Roxanne Kent wrote television documentaries on environmental issues, and consulted with clients from government agencies to sponsors of political referendums. She has written lyrics, books, and plays for children and continues to serve as a lay leader in her church and community.

***

Sundays at Ebenezer held a cherished constant - lively discussions in the Sunday school class taught for many years by my wonderfully loving teacher, Daisy Allman. We explored all sorts of Bible stories, often exploring their relevance to contemporary life.

I was a frequent challenger in those spirited debates and even at a young age could appreciate her tolerance and encouragement of sharp questioning. It is true that my theology is now markedly different from the more literal interpretations held by many in the church at that time, but the love and sense of family that she and so many of the wonderful members showed, and the sense of Christ as a chosen path have been a lifelong strength, and those early, never dull exchanges helped me grow more secure in coming to my own independent journey of faith and affirmed the message..."and the greatest of these is love".

Legacies

In Memoriam - Harlem

Here are some of the now deceased members of <u>Harlem</u> Ebenezer who were active during the first 50 years:[49]

VERNICE ALLEYNE	ROSALIE FAGAN
VERONICA ALLEYNE	CAROLINE FARNUM
REV. CHARLES E. ALLMAN	EDITH FARNUM
CYNTHIA ALLMAN	REV. E. EUSTACE FARNUM
DAISY ALLMAN	CLARA FARNUM
DORIS ALLMAN	HOPE FARNUM
FELIX ALLMAN	EDITH FOSTER
REV. LUTHER ALLMAN	SYBIL GARNES
MABEL ALLMAN	MALVINA GILL
MIRIAM ALLMAN	ALDWIN GRANDERSON
DOROTHY BARTLETT	LORNA GRANDERSON
DORCAS BOWEN	LEONARD GRANT, SR.
EVA BOWEN	LORETTA GREAVES
KETURAH BOWEN	WILLIAM GREEN, CHARTER MEMBER
INEZ BURROWS	
MAUDE BURROWS	BEATRICE GREENIDGE
HENRY FAGAN	EDMUND GREENIDGE

JAMES GREENIDGE	ANNIE MCLEAN
LEACHMAN GREENIDGE	ESTHER MILLER
LUCILLE GREENIDGE	GWENDOLYN MORGAN
RALPH GREENIDGE	LYDIA MORGAN
HOWARD HARRIS	RACHEL MORGAN
REBECCA HARRIS	REV. SAMUEL MORGAN
YVONNE MILLER HAZEL	ELIZABETH NEMBLETT
CHRISTOPHER HINDS	JEMIMA NESFIELD
IVY HINDS	MIRIAM RAMSAY
ALBERTA HOGAN	JANE RASMUSSEN
REV. GEORGE HOLDER	CAROLINE SANDIFORD
MILLICENT HOWELL	RUTH SEALE
KETURAH ISAAC	REV. ARCHIE SHEPHERD
ARNOLD JONES	SYLVIA ALLMAN SHEPHERD
SAMUEL KIRTON	BEATRICE SMITH
CAROLINE KIRTON	CATHERINE SMITH
CHARLES LASHLEY	REV. H.F. SMITH
GOLDIE LUKE	HENRIETTA SMITH
INEZ LUKE	WINIFRED SMITH
MARY MAXWELL	NOREEN WALL
ALBERTHA MCHARDY	SIMEON WALL

STONE OF HELP

ELLA WATERMAN

EUNICE WATERMAN

JANE WATERMAN

ORLANDO WATERMAN

MILLICENT WHARTON

JAMES W. WHEATLEY

MARY WHEATLEY

REV. CLEMENT WHITEHEAD

MAUDE WHITEHEAD

In Memoriam – Brooklyn

Here are some of the now deceased members of <u>Brooklyn</u> Ebenezer who were active during the first 50 years

LEON ADAMS	MURIEL GREENIDGE
RUTH ALLEYNE	LOUISE HARDING
LILLIAN BLACKMAN	ISABELE HAZELEY
HORTENSE BOYCE	JAMES HOLLINSWORTH
LUCRETIA BRADFORD	MARION HOLLINSWORTH
FRANK BURKE	MARJORIE HUMPHREY
ALFRED CALLENDER	ARNOLD JOHNSON
DOROTHY CARRINGTON	SARAH JOHNSON
MELVENA CHANDLER	MACNEIL JORDAN
MIRIAM FOSTER	ARNOLD JOHNSON
REV. PERCY GADSBY	DARNLEY JOHNSON
REV. LESTER GIBBS	LOUISE KNIGHT
CLARA GREAVES	RHODA LEWIS
GRAZELDA GREAVES	ELEASE MOE
IRVINE GREAVES	GEORGE OTTLEY
FITZ GREEN	SUSAN OTTLEY
LILLIAN GREENIDGE	KATHLEEN RISBROOK

STONE OF HELP

MIRIAM RISBROOK

AARON SKEETE

MILDRED SMALL

EUDORA ST. HILL

HAROLD ST. HILL

JOSEPHINE TULLE

EVERARD WAITHE

JONATHAN WALTERS

ALMA YEARWOOD

AUBREY YEARWOOD

Living Hall of Fame

Below are the names of some of those who attended Ebenezer in the first 50 years, who are still alive, and some of the contributions they have made to society. The omission of other individuals is due only to the fact that we were unable to contact them:

Luther Allman, Jr
. Retired corporate officer; Organist

Dr. Grace Allman Burke
Retired Certified Nurse Midwife; Ordained minister

Dr. Ronald Brown
Psychologist

Hon. Carl O. Callender
Retired judge; Associate Pastor

Cecilia Denise Callender
Certified Substance Abuse Counselor; Church deacon

Dr. Clive O. Callender
Kidney transplant surgeon; university professor

Lenora Wheatley Cooper
Retired nurse

Gloria Callender Doyle
Retired school principal

Olwen Allman Gillman
Retired beautician; Church lay leader

Henry Granderson
    Retired

Rev. Henry Greenidge
    Pastor

Ralph Greenidge, Jr.
    Retired Police Officer

Gloria Wheatley Johnson
    Retired Assistant Principal

Roxanne Johnson Kent
    Writer, Church Deacon

Marilyn Allman Maye, Ed.D.
    University professor; Church deacon

Rev. Gloria W. Nurse
    Ordained minister; Associate Pastor

Dorothy Oliver
    Retired missionary

Edith Farnum Rock
    Retired nurse; college professor

Waldo Waterman
    Retired printer; Church soloist

Photographs

A 1930s photograph of the Sunday School children of the Ebenezer Gospel Tabernacle of the Christian Mission of the U.S.A., with Elder Farnum standing on the right side. Several of the children in this picture are still alive today, and are in their eighties and nineties. Among them still living are Gloria Wheatley Johnson, Lenora Wheatley Cooper, Olwen Allman Gilman, and Eileen Armstrong. The photograph was taken outside of the West 127th Street church location, later sold when they moved to Lenox Avenue.[50]

The photograph above shows several of the ministers of the church, including an aged Elder Farnum (seated), shortly before his death in 1952. Standing, from left to right are: Revs. Charles Allman, Vincent Griffiths, Ralph Greenidge, George Simpson, Luther Allman, Archibald Shepherd and Clement Whitehead. None of the persons in this photo is alive today.

Excerpt from *New York Amsterdam News*, October 24, 1928[51]

The Rev. B. Farnum, who conducts services in a private house at 15 West 127th street, was summoned Friday before Magistrate Rosenbluth in Harlem Court on a charge of conducting a public nuisance.

The minister was arraigned on complaint of Mr. and Mrs. Joseph W. Savage, white, 13 West 127th street. They were accompanied by several other white tenants, all of whom complained that their sleep was disturbed by the noises made during the services.

Savage testified that since last August he and the other tenants have been annoyed by noises made in the improvised church, where nightly services are held, sometimes as late as midnight. These services are held with the aid of musical instruments, consisting of an organ, a piano and several horns, Savage said.

"They stamp their feet, clap their hands and go crazy," Mrs. Savage told the Magistrate.

The Rev. Mr. Farnum testified he was a regular ordained minister of the gospel and has been one for thirty-one years. His church, he said, has been conducting services in Harlem for the past seventeen years. He denied that the services lasted later than 10:30 p. m., adding that although complaints had been made to the police they had investigated and had found no cause for complaint.

The Magistrate adjourned the case, and in the meantime an investigation is to be made by a probation officer.

Afterword

My hope is that this retrospective will renew interest in the values and contributions of those who founded Ebenezer, to the benefit of present and future generations.

As the 1960s dawned, my peers began to enter our young adult years. By that time, more and more members of the church were living outside of Harlem, driving in from Queens, the Bronx and Brooklyn. The American-born offspring of the founding immigrants were branching out.

From the perspective of the founders, if they were here today, they would see many successes, as well as some casualties of their migration to Harlem. As the memoirs show, several of their descendants became leaders in other church organizations. Their places back home were taken by a new wave of immigrants from the Caribbean who came in the 60 and 70s. These newer families are represented among those who remain in Ebenezer as of the centennial year. They have brought their own gifts, experienced new successes, and further expanded the church's influence in the world.

On the other hand, some of the successive generations came to look down on their parents' church culture. Adopting mainstream lifestyles, they married people with different religious convictions;

they served in the military and experienced disillusionment; they became exposed to the business world, and got caught in unethical practices; some slipped into drug abuse and alcoholism.

If the founders could preview the next 50 years, what would they see? The answers to that question will emerge from the decisions that are made today.

I hope these memoirs will stimulate younger researchers to capture more of the stories and contributions of persons from all eras who built Ebenezer Gospel Tabernacle and left a rich heritage for future generations. Whatever form the future takes, I hope that Ebenezer will always maintain a commitment to the urban communities where we grew up. I hope that each of us will continually pray and work for both spiritual revival as well as social and economic justice, in our communities, and wherever God will use the Ebenezer legacy around the world.

Marilyn C. Maye Ed.D.
June, 2011

The editor, a lifelong educator, has co-authored with her husband, Warren L Maye, *Orita: Rites of Passage for Youth of African Descent in America* (New York: FaithWorks, 2000). *Orita* rites of passage provide a forum for transmitting to the next generation the history, spiritual values, and life skills that children of the African Diaspora will always need to thrive in a race-conscious society. More information is available at www.oritaritesofpassage.org

Notes

[1] http://history1900s.about.com/od/1900s/qt/licenseplates.htm (accessed May 1, 2011).

[2] http://history1900s.about.com/od/1900s/qt/naacp.htm (accessed May 1, 2011).

[3] http://en.wikipedia.org/wiki/Triangle_Shirtwaist_Factory_fire (accessed May 29, 2011).

[4] http://www.columbia.edu/cu/iraas/harlem/neighborhood/battle.html (accessed May 6, 2011).

[5] *A brief outline of the history of the Christian Mission of the U.S.A. 50th Anniversary Journal of the Christian Mission of the USA, 1911 - 1961.*

[6] Bureau of Census, *Negro Population of the United States,* 1790-1915 (Washington, D.C.: Government Printing Office 1918), 61

[7] W. James, *The History of Afro-Caribbean Migration to the United States* (New York: Columbia University), http://www.inmotionaame.org/texts/viewer.cfm?id=10_000T&page=1 (accessed on April 28, 2011).

[8] Ibid.
[9] Ibid.
[10] Ibid.
[11] Ibid.

[12] The New Testament gospel of Mark quotes Jesus as warning about this in chapter 8 verse 36 through 38.

[13] I. Wilkerson, *The Warmth of Other Suns: The Epic Story of America's Great Migration* (New York: Random House, 2010). Census records of the time show a greater percentage of blacks from the South had completed high school than had those born in many northern cities. More marriages among the migrants were intact.

[14] J. N. Gregory, *The Southern Diaspora: How the Great Migrations of Black and White Southerners Transformed America* (Chapel Hill: University of North Carolina Press, 2005).

[15] http://en.wikipedia.org/wiki/Paul_Robeson (accessed May 6, 2011)

[16] http://en.wikipedia.org/wiki/Percy_Sutton (accessed May 6, 2011)

[17] http://www.wheaton.edu/bgc/archives/trans/430t01.htm (accessed May 6, 2011)

[18] Wilkerson, *op. cit.*

[19] Reading back issues of Jet magazine provides rich detail on activities in churches like Mt. Morris Presbyterian. In November, 1965, the pastor, Rev. Eugene Adair, married singer Leslie Uggams to an Australian in a ceremony at the church. These stories reveal the type of social class represented in the congregation at that time.

[20] http://www.nacog.com/site/AboutNACOG/History/tabid/138/Default.aspx (accessed on May 28, 2011).

[21] http://www.nacog.com/site/AboutNACOG/History/tabid/138/Default.aspx (accessed on May 9, 2011).

[22] In an October 17, 1959 edition of the *New York Amsterdam News* a photograph appears showing Harlem ministers participating in the 150th Anniversary Clergy Committee of the New York Bible Society, launching weekly Bible readings in their churches. The clergy were renown leaders of the era; listed with their organizations, they were Reverends: V. Simpson Turner, NY Bible Society; Lovelle Maxwell, Mt. Olivet Baptist Church; M. L. Wilson, Convent Avenue Baptist Church; Charles Warren, St. Marks Church; Einslow Beckles, Fourth Moravian Church; David Bruno, Thomas Memorial Wesleyan; Major B. Barton McIntrye, Salvation Army; Luther Allman, Ebenezer gospel Tabernacle; S. B. Joubert, Baptist Ministers Conference; J. Franklin Smith, Church on the Hill; W. Sterling Cary, Grace Congregational ; H. Arthur Doughlin, St. Luke's. The editor notes that no women are among them. (ProQuest Historical Newspapers *New York Amsterdam News: 1922 - 1993*).

[23] *Jet magazine*, June 20, 1963

[24] *New York Amsterdam News*. (1957, February 2). "Radio Show Tests Youth's Bible Info." ProQuest Historical newspapers New York Amsterdam News: 1922 - 1993. Bible quizzes were aired on WWRL on Sunday evenings at 9:45 during the 1950s and 60s.

[25] *Ibid*. A photograph is shown of "Bible experts," Luther Allman and Clive Callender, representing Ebenezer, competing against a team from Ephesus SDA church, in the radio station studio in 1957.

[26] http://northbysouth.kenyon.edu/1998/death/mickey%27s.htm (accessed on May 28, 2011).

[27] http://www.thewoodlawncemetery.org/africanamerican.html (accessed on May 28, 2011). The cemetery's website contains a treasure trove of information about the black history greats buried there: including Nobel Peace Prize winner Ralph Bunche and economist Dr. William Henry Dean; Harlem Renaissance poet Countee Cullen; musicians W. C. Handy, Coleman Hawkins, and Miles Davis; millionaire entrepreneur Madam C.J.Walker, and Broadway actress and film star, Hilda Haynes, *nee* Lashley, herself a child of Ebenezer.

[28] The editor's mother and father were from these different versions of the "Christian Mission." On a visit to Panama in 2007, the editor discovered a small museum memorializing blacks who helped build the Panama Canal. The museum is housed in the former church building of the Christian Mission of Panama, of which my maternal grandfather was a founding member.

[29] M. B. Richardson, "Brooklyn Church Bulletin," *New York Amsterdam News,* December 15, 1945. (ProQuest Historical Newspapers *New York Amsterdam News: 1922 - 1993).*

[30] http://www.adventistcolleges.org/CMSColleges.asp?CollegeID=15 (accessed on May 28, 2011).

[31] http://en.wikipedia.org/wiki/Wintley_Phipps and http://en.wikipedia.org/wiki/Take_6 (accessed on May 28, 2011).

[32] W. L. Maye, *Soldiers of Uncommon Valor: The History of Salvationists of African Descent in the United States* (New York: Others Press, 2008).

[33] Ibid.

[34] B. Sherrod, A tribute to the late Bishop Caesar, *Love Express*, http://loveexpressonline.com/roderickcaesar.html (accessed on May 17, 2011)

[35] http://www.huffingtonpost.com/eddie-glaude-jr-phd/the-black-church-is-dead_b_473815.html (accessed on May 9, 2011).

[36] http://www.youtube.com/IraasColumbia (accessed on May 9, 2011)

[37] These stories are found in the books of Genesis, chapters 37 – 50; Exodus, chapters 1 – 15; and Esther, chapters 2 – 10.

[38] See the Old Testament's First Book of Samuel, chapter 7, where the events leading up to the mention of *Ebenezer* in scripture.

[39] The King James Version of the Bible translates Samuel's statement as "Hitherto hath the Lord helped us." That wording has been memorialized in the lyrics of the hymn, *"Here I raise my Ebenezer; Hither by Thy help I've come; And I hope, by Thy good pleasure, Safely to arrive at home."* (Attributed to Robert Robinson, 1758, (according to http://nethymnal.org/htm/c/o/comethou.htm).

[40] http://en.wikipedia.org/wiki/William_Wilberforce (accessed on May 6, 2011)

[41] http://www.chog.org/AboutUs/OurHistory/tabid/67/Default.aspx (accessed on May 9, 2011).

[42] http://en.wikipedia.org/wiki/Church_of_God_(Cleveland,_Tennessee) (accessed on May 9, 2011).

[43] http://www.wheaton.edu/bgc/archives/docs/waite.htm (accessed on May 3, 2011).

[44] Personal communication from Dr. Grace Allman Burke, on May 27, 2011. She remembers Rev. Waite staying at the Allman's home when he was back in the States on furlough.

[45] W. Jones, *Living in Two Worlds* (Grand Rapids, MI: Zondervan Publishers, 1988), http://www.ccel.us/wandajones.ch3.html (accessed May 3, 2011).

[46] Two articles from the New York Amsterdam News dated October 24, 1928 and July 15, 1931, describe both the worship practices of holiness churches like Ebenezer, as well as the reactions from their contemporaries, white and black, who found them most unusual.

[47] Rev. Farnum remained as Superintendent over the two churches for another two years.

[48] "Advancing arms" refers to an activity during which participants stood erect, extending their arms with Bibles in hand. The Bibles contained the Word of God, an offensive weapon in spiritual warfare, as per Ephesians chapter 6.

[49] This is not a definitive list and does not include many members of the Brooklyn church, who also had a major impact on the lives of those who contributed to this project.

[50] Photograph copied from the private collection of Dr. Grace Allman Burke.

[51] "White Tenants Hale Preacher to Court." *New York Amsterdam News,* October 24, 1928. (ProQuest Historical Newspapers New York Amsterdam News, 1922-1993).

www.ingramcontent.com/pod-product-compliance
Lightning Source LLC
Chambersburg PA
CBHW020008050426
42450CB00005B/370